SUPERSTORM SANDY:
A Diary in the Dark

BY

WILLIAM WESTHOVEN

OTHER BOOKS BY WILLIAM WESTHOVEN:

Fiction:
"One-Hit Willie: A Classic Rock Novel" (2011)
"The Puddingstone Well" (2012)

Nonfiction:
"Eric Clapton: Career of a Rock Legend" (1996)

For more information and updates:
visit www.onehitwillie.com
or the "Superstorm Sandy: A Diary in the Dark" page on Facebook.

DEDICATION

To my wife and occasional editor, Lisa, for her tight deadline editing, her body heat and for teaching me how to fry lasagna.

ACKNOWLEDGMENTS

Special thanks to the first responders, both our local public servants and those who came from all over North America to help us in our most significant time of need. Also to the many friends, family and others who offered to share their homes with us while ours was frozen over. Thanks to the Red Cross for being there, as they always are, and for all the volunteers who pitched in and made a difference. Their work is not done, of course, and I'm hoping the funds raised from this book will help New Jersey and its brave, hearty residents to finish the job.

INTRODUCTION: Hello, My Name is Bill W.

Wrapped in more layers than a ripe Spanish onion —
with an aroma to match — I woke in my own bed bearing
witness to my own breath. I summoned my microscopic
reserve of resolve, slipped out from under a half-dozen
mismatched bedcovers and trudged slowly to the bathroom,
wondering how cold the toilet seat was today.

I stood in front of the mirror, even though first light
had not quite found the window. I was little more than a
shadow, a hulking silhouette with unruly geysers of hair
exploding from my head.

Does this make me look fat? I wondered, stuffing two
long-sleeve shirts into my heavy cotton sweatpants and letting
two more hang over.

*You are fat, and you're wearing four heavy pullovers, so
yeah, it's not a good look for you,* I replied. Maybe I said it out
loud, and maybe I didn't. There was no one around to hear.
My secret was safe a while longer.

It was a Casual Friday morning, Day 12 of my
Superstorm Sandy imprisonment. Before this goes any further,
I should make it clear that my personal storm-survival
experience was inconsequential by the adjusted standards of
living we found ourselves immersed in following the worst
natural disaster ever to hit New Jersey and our neighbors in
New York.

Safely removed from the unimaginable horror at the
Jersey Shore, where the tidal surge wiped out so many homes,
boardwalks and cherished summer memories, we were at first
counting ourselves among the lucky up in North Jersey.
Sandy's crocodile tears dropped less than two inches of rain
on us over about 24 hours.

We can do two inches standing on our head and breathing through a straw. It was only last year that a series of relentless spring floods preceded the August arrival of Hurricane Irene, which flooded our usual risk areas along with other places we always thought could hold their water.

Then there was the Halloween Blizzard, which sprayed heavy snow and ice into defenseless trees that had yet to drop their leaves. Instead, the trees themselves dropped, creating what some local utilities referred to as the third 100-year storm of 2011.

Both Irene and the Octoblizzard caused widespread power failures, too, but even the worst-hit areas had their lines restored in less than a week. My wife and I were mostly fortunate that year. After some basement flooding in the spring, we had a sump pump installed and it kept the Irene flooding to a minimum.

"Of course, what good is the sump pump if the power goes out?" my wife, Lisa, said.

Yeah, but we dropped nearly three large on the sump-pump installation, just a few months before both of us were laid off. So we put off the generator, vowing it would be our first major purchase when we got back to full-time work.

Which we have not yet managed to do. I'm a journalist, for criminy sake. The current job market treats over-50 journalists such as myself like flood-soaked Drywall.

Did I mention 2011 sucked? But at least the power stayed on, although a few scattered outages gave us pause.

Not this time, buster.

Irene nearly drowned our beloved Garden State, but once the flood waters receded after a few short days, we were able to dry off, clean up and get back to business.

Wind damage is a different beast. When a windstorm is over, the trees, poles and lines don't just pop back up. Nor do they drag themselves off your roads, your vehicles … or your dwellings … or empty themselves into streams and drains.

Sandy blew with the vengeance of a jilted lover, her blind fury growing throughout the night as though she were popping transformers like five-hour energy drinks. Her path of destruction was as indiscriminate as a rubber-suited Japanese movie monster, leaving some heels and toes of the neighborhood flattened like a footprint while nearby homes were completely spared.

Except, of course, for the power lines, phone lines and cable lines. Strung on wooden poles lined up like street-side dominoes and fatally tethered to each other, a near-miss from a windstorm is as good as a direct hit. If you were upriver, so to speak, from a downed line, you were screwed.

And in many areas, there were trees, poles and lines down on every other street.

In the most densely populated of these United States.

Getting the picture?

I'm sure many of you followed Superstorm Sandy on the news and are acutely aware that it was a tempest for the ages. More than 100 lives were lost and the estimated costs — topping $30 billion in both New York *and* New Jersey — ranks it just below Hurricane Katrina as the most devastating storm in modern history.

Of course, this is not a competition. We understand the immensity of Katrina and believe me, we are grateful Sandy did not clear the bar she set, particularly in the category of human lives. But just like Katrina and its challenging aftermath, we here in the Tristate are experiencing feelings that you cannot possibly imagine unless you were here. We are feeling flood-level pangs of loss and anger; high tides of fear, sadness and anxiety; we are in some cases considering or reconsidering our very mortality.

All that and we endured some really bad hair days, at least in my case.

So while my wife and I were quite lucky by comparison, I felt compelled to share my Sandy story with three goals in mind. One is to help those who were not here —

and wish to understand — by sharing my experience and whatever perspective comes with it. The second goal is to submit my account to all those who were here and wish to bounce their perspective off my own, compare their experience to mine and learn they are not alone in their confusion and suffering.

Misery loves company, that's what they say, right? And superstorms make strange bedfellows. I once had an uncle who was fond of saying that. Or maybe it was me. Hard to say. Less than a month after Sandy struck, I am still a little disoriented.

I offer my story and perspective with the experience of a longtime local newspaper journalist who has reported on many storms over the last two decades, but none that packed the wallop of the wrathful Sandy. I also bought the house I grew up in here in Parsippany and Morris County, a typically crowded suburban tangle of commerce and bedroom communities, so I know my way around, even in the dead dark and with half the roads blocked by high-voltage debris.

Finally, I'm hoping to turn this chickenshit event into chicken salad by donating my royalties from this eBook to the Hurricane Sandy New Jersey Relief Fund. So if you enjoy my little story, please help the cause and recommend it to a friend. Or a bunch of friends. And all those people you friended on Facebook even though you really don't like them. And if you don't like this book, well, recommend it anyway. Don't harsh my fundraising mellow.

In the effort to publish this book while the topic is still fresh in my mind — and my story can be put to the most timely use — you may find a few extra typos here and there. Get over it. This is a fund-raiser. Dogging me about typos would be like criticizing the quality of the Sunday gravy at the Legion Hall spaghetti dinner. The money you pay will go to a good cause and you'll leave with a full belly, so hush up and eat.

Why the Hurricane Sandy New Jersey Relief Fund? Since its founding by New Jersey First Lady Mary Pat Christie, the fund has raised millions for the direct benefit of my beloved Garden State. I am very grateful to the Red Cross for its help during the crisis, but with the wounds from this disaster still so very fresh, it's hard for me to look past our state borders.

Along the way, I'll share some of the drama and hopefully some of the lighter moments, those "you have to laugh to keep from crying" scenarios that sustained us in our darkest hours, and believe me, there were plenty of those, metaphorical and otherwise.

Some of the dialogue will be transcripted from my social-media network. With no TV, cable or internet, my iPhone became a lifeline, connecting me to an improvised support group of close and casual friends who banded together and conspired to keep me sane. I hope I returned the favor with some of the humor I've been known for (or accused of) and by force-feeding a positive attitude that I felt we might need should the worst happen, which by most measures turned out to be the case.

I embark on this literary journey less than three days after getting my power back on November 9, with the goal of publishing while the subject of Sandy is still fresh in our minds. Soon enough, we will forget Sandy and banish her to the far recesses of our memory. Put her out of sight and out of mind, at least until we've had a chance to rest and heal.

But there is so much to learn from the bumper crop of life experience we just harvested. We've learned so much already, about ourselves, our climate, our infrastructure and our neighbors, both the ones in our neighborhood and the army of first-responder linemen who were welcomed like the Sicilians cheered Patton's Seventh Army when it rolled into Palermo.

So I write to remember and hopefully you will read … and learn … and remember … and know what to expect when the water rises, the air turns sideways and the walls come tumbling down.

PROLOGUE: The Piggys in the Brick House

"When a tropical system combines with a cold system, we call it an atmospheric bomb." — Sam Champion, senior weather editor, ABC News, Monday, October 29, 2012

How many times had we heard this before?

"There's a storm coming, a big one, maybe THE big one," was the consensus of the weather forecasters in print, online and on the airwaves.

Granted, those weather geeks are pretty good at their job. In fact, we usually get more than four days warning, but there were several fronts and factors in play, forming a weather model that had some of the most experienced meteorologists claiming they had never seen anything like it. An arctic blast from the northwest smacking upside a tropical storm right on the Jetstream running through the most populous corridor of our nation.

All this with a nor'easter that was practically tailgating the tropical storm, which matured into Hurricane Sandy before it hit Jamaica and Cuba.

OK, fine, we all know what to do — rush to the supermarket and buy all the bottled water, milk and liquor we can fit into our vehicles. What is it about the prospect of flooding that compels us to fill our homes with more liquid?

Another day passes and the weather geeks are sounding increasingly worried and confused. Usually, when a storm is tracking just as they predicted, they strut like peacocks, their body language practically screaming "I told you so." This time around, however, there is more sweating than strutting. Sandy is one crazy bitch, they admit, and there's no telling what she is capable of, only that nothing good will come of her visit.

Another day passes, we're into the weekend and Sandy's ETA is adjusted to Monday-Tuesday. Our bigger-than-life governor, Chris Christie, is on the job. He got caught at Disney World during the 2010 Christmas blizzard and is too smart to make that mistake a second time. Breathing heavily into the microphones, he takes appropriate charge of the situation, orders evacuations of barrier islands and warns people to prepare for the worst.

The people listen, Democrats and Republicans of one voice for a change on the cusp of a contentious presidential election. We listen, and head back to the store for more liquid.

My wife and I smile confidently. We stock up on sales and have a full pantry, fridge and basement freezer. We don't fear tap water and we really don't indulge in alcohol. We were the piggys in the brick house. We know how to weather a storm. If things go bad and we are stranded for a few days, we have it covered. Our greatest fear is losing power to the sump pump should our flood-prone basement start to take on water.

We briefly discuss going out and overpaying for a generator, but again, money is tight and besides, they probably were sold out already, so why bother? If it gets too bad, we can call the fire department and they will come and pump it out. They are pretty good about that.

And hey, the weather geeks keep saying they have never seen a storm like this one, so what do they really know, anyway? We could end up with an Indian Summer for all they know.

We cross into Monday and the governor is still huffing, puffing and warning us to pay attention. It's cool, Chris, we hear you. Big storm. Stay home tonight.

"I feel like the disaster governor," Christie says with a chuckle, referring to the 2011 storms and tossing out a straight line to liberal comics from coast to coast.

The weather geeks, though, have me worried. Some of them are looking pale and nervous, like they are looking for a back exit out of the studio and an escape route to higher ground. The wife and I do a revised inventory. We have plenty of flashlights, but not as many batteries as we thought. And some of the older flashlights are dimming already.

Fine, swell, we still have candles. That's how they did it in the Olden Days, right? Good enough for the Continental Congress, good enough for us.

I pause to regret not stopping to gas up my car, but I have close to half a tank and why am I worrying about gas, anyway? What could possibly happen that might require extra gas?

As the day progresses, the forecasters narrow their focus. The good news is that North Jersey may not get the rain one might expect from a superstorm, two to four inches most of them said. That was within our estimated basement tolerance, so no worries there.

The real alarm, at least for us in North Jersey, are the wind advisories, which ranged from as high as 50 to 90 miles per hour. We live on a small quarter acre packed with a dozen fully grown trees. Our shoulder-rubbing neighbors on each side have their fair share as well. Sooner or later, we were destined to lose the tree lottery.

I watch another forecaster as she ties back her hair, puts on her slicker and goes outside to do a remote. A fairly light rain begins around lunchtime and the winds swiftly follow, turning the precipitation into an annoying spritz.

Midway through the afternoon, the lights flicker, followed by a surprisingly early blackout. *Really?* Not much of a storm yet, hard to imagine things would deteriorate so quickly.

The power pops back on about three minutes later. *That's more like it.* Just a little scare. Gets our attention, though, and once the DVR completes its familiar, annoyingly long reboot, we commit our attention to local TV news, which had all switched over to full-time storm coverage. Never a good sign when they do that, although the talking heads have jumped the gun more than once in the past. So a bad storm was not yet *fait accompli*, but since they are making the effort to cover it without commercial interruption, we figure that watching was the least we could do. They might come in handy later on. And watching some of those knuckleheads hanging onto boardwalk rails for dear life during Hurricane Irene was quite entertaining.

And "Katie" was pre-empted, anyway, so what the hey?

I jest. We are already watching. I may be laid off from my newspaper job, but I'm still a news junkie. And storm-watching is embedded in my DNA. My father loved a good storm and threw himself into weather preparations the minute Dr. Frank Field would sound the alarm on the Six O'Clock News. Back in the day, when 24-hour TV news was as unknown to Ted Turner as his third wife, Dad would switch from TV to radio and from Dr. Frank Field to Dr. Bob Harris, the WCBS-AM news radio weatherman who, as it turned out, wasn't really a doctor. My father never forgave Dr. Bob for breaching the sacred weatherman-weatherfan bond.

Whenever a big storm is brewing, I always remember my Dad and how much fun he had, rubbing his hands together in warm anticipation of a good old-fashioned hunker-down.

Of course, it's all fun and games until the world knocks on your door and says, "you won't be needing that pilot light for a while."

DAY 1: Dinner by Candlelight

"More than a million customers already were without power by early evening and millions more could lose electricity. One disaster forecasting company predicted economic losses could ultimately reach $20 billion, only half of it insured." — Reuters report, 7:54 p.m. Monday, October 29, 2012

I was making dinner when our light, heat and communications were cut off around 6:30 p.m.

Minute steaks. I was cooking minute steaks. Seemed like a good idea at the time, a simple meal from a full freezer, some cheese, bread and ketchup. Quick and easy comfort food. It appeared we would have a long night ahead of us as the winds graduated from howls to roars.

We turned up the TV to drown out the noise outside. It was bad enough that you could feel it, even behind four sturdy walls — window frames clicking, foundation rumbling, debris rapping and smashing against the vinyl siding, like the second half of an extended John Bonham drum solo, when he would just stagger around and look for something else to bang on.

Yeah, I saw Led Zeppelin in concert. They were pretty damn loud.

So was Sandy. We raised the volume on News 12 and focused on dinner.

The minute steaks turned out to be a bad idea. Now, I know they are processed, but when you take them out of the package, they look so clean and uniformly red, like razor-thin slices of the leanest beef you could possibly imagine. Not a trace of fat in sight. You figure the cattle they carve them from must run marathons or something.

Then you cook them and they all but disappear under their own grease. And you stare down at your pan, fooled once again, and wonder what number of red dye they pump into those beef shingles that melt into beef broth right before your eyes.

None of which is your problem, but the physical and chemical composition of the minute steaks became the first of our Superstorm Sandy-related problems.

Shrinkage notwithstanding, dinner preparations were on schedule and according to plan when the power died at — what did I say before? — six-thirty? Yeah, it was right about 6:30 and just as the minute steaks began to shrink, they disappeared completely.

Along with the rest of the kitchen.

Fortunately, our kitchen island had been designated as Flashlight Central, so I managed to quickly switch on a LED lantern and regain my culinary bearings. The minute steaks were building up quite an oil reserve and would be done in, well, surely less than a minute.

I turned my attention to the ultimate destination of the minute steaks, the four slices of my wife's yummy home-made bread. All standing patiently in the toaster, waiting to accept our desired crispness.

I should confess. The wife's home-made bread is indeed tasty, but somewhat dense, especially when it was cold. The prospect of eating the minute steaks on untoasted white bread was a tangible disappointment.

It was the first of many disappointments headed our way.

I thought about grilling the bread but the minute steaks were not going to wait. So I sighed, put the cold bread on two plates and tried my best to make the sandwiches without spilling the wading pool of grease in the pan. Limited to a narrow beam of light and needing two hands for my job, drippings and spillings landed on the counter, floor and the stove, causing a split-second flare of fire.

Less than one minute steak into the greatest power outage in New Jersey history, we were already experiencing potentially dangerous domestic complications. We ate silently, leaving cold-bread crusts on our plates. We had misplaced our appetites somewhere in the darkness.

Lisa lit some candles, backlighting Flashlight Central, which looked a little like a scale model of New York skyscrapers with the sun rising behind them. Normally, a candlelight dinner and a view of the Manhattan skyline might strike a romantic mood, but with a superstorm at our door, and grease on our floor, our baser instincts were preoccupied with the kind of uncertainty that darkness demands.

We used a match to relight the stove burner and boiled some water to wash the dishes. We left the grease on the floor for daylight. We'd give the kitchen and the house a good cleaning as soon as the lights came back on in a few hours … a few days? Who knew? But our previous power losses had all been measured in hours, not days … or weeks. We had no reason to think this blackout would be any different, although it was a safe bet we would be out until the storm passed and the sun rose.

After dinner, we settled back into the living room in front of the TV, mainly out of habit. Lisa used the little LED lantern to light her early-generation Kindle. She wasn't one for technology but she loves her Kindle and had downloaded plenty of titles.

I caressed my iPhone and jumped on Facebook to check out the chatter. The screen glowed cheerfully but it could not connect to the Internet. Had a cell tower lost power, or perhaps even blown over? There always had been a healthy signal here.

It had a full battery charge, game apps and a Kindle app with full access to Lisa's library, so the iPhone was still my refuge, but it was troubling to consider a near future without the ability to communicate. For a news junkie, that's like cutting off Donald Trump from his hairspray.

16

Then I remembered my little portable radio, a free gift redeemed through reward points from a credit card I no longer possessed. Operating on four AA batteries, it was roughly the size of a Subway Five-Dollar Footlong, with little removable speakers on each side. The Visa gift catalog described it as a portable stereo, and I suppose that was technically accurate, but when it arrived, its blurry molded plastic and tinny sound mocked me to the point that I almost threw it out. Over time, it proved to be reliable, easily stored and generally handy, despite its utter inability to live up to the catalog promise.

And in the dark, its lack of switches, dials and controls proved to be a godsend. I didn't need tone adjustments to listen to news radio on AM. On, off, AM, FM, station dial and volume. That's all I needed to assume control.

I switched on the radio and tuned in my Dad's old standby, WCBS News Radio 880. Funny how I recognized many of the announcer voices but could never remember their names, with the possible exception of Dr. Bob, who of course was long gone.

"We are getting reports of significant power outages by the local utilities," the announcer said.

No shit.

He also passed along some incomplete but dreadful reports of massive flooding in Atlantic City and the barrier islands of the Jersey Shore. By this time, though, some of the knucklehead boardwalks had already been torn up and were floating inland, so the kind of eyewitness reports we received during Hurricane Irene were in short supply. And by this time, it was darker than the governor's exercise room out there, so we realized it would be morning before we got many details about the destruction already in progress.

We both chewed on our ebooks for another hour or two, pausing with readers on our chests whenever Sandy cleared her throat and exhaled. The full moon gave the ferocious night sky a dim, eerie glow, just enough that you could see the treetops bowing to their new mistress, imploring her not to bring them to their knees. Some, as we would learn, were spared. Many others would not be. For now, the culling had just begun. All any of us could do now was sit and wait.

Surrendering to our wide-ranging helplessness, we decided to turn in early. The forecasters were predicting the winds would ease overnight and by about 3 a.m., the worst would be over. Might was well sleep through the peak storm hours and rest up for what promised to be a busy morning.

The house was still warm, but we huddled closer than usual that night in bed, taking comfort in our still-functioning bodies, fully fueled on minute steaks and prepared to burn calories at least until breakfast.

Outside, Sandy had raised the volume of her ground assault. Or perhaps it was just the deafening silence in a bedroom where we usually fell asleep to the TV, surrounded by glowing digital readouts and status lights on cable boxes, phones and all the other devices we depend so much on to connect our lives to the world around us. We still had each other, but with so many of our familiar visual and auditory markers missing in action, the storm grew louder and louder … almost as loud as our pounding hearts.

DAY 2: The New Normal

" ... Limited restoration today. We will begin restoring power tomorrow after we assess." — JCP&L representative, Tuesday, October 30, 2012

When we woke at first light, the world around us had mercifully stopped spinning. After a night with temperatures in the 40s, the thermostat read 69 degrees. Our humble split level had lost some color from its cheeks, but 69 was tolerable. As long as we had power back before dark, we would be back to near normal by dinnertime.

Absorbing the sober radio reports emanating from the Jersey Shore, and having glanced out windows in four directions, it appeared we had dodged the bullet outside as well. Now it was time to go out there and see for myself.

One of the decorative shutters had blown off its mooring alongside our living-room picture window. Our Rubbermaid mini-shed out back also lost a door, coincidentally about the same size as the picture-window shutter. I looked around. Both slabs of plastic were, to coin a phrase, gone with the wind.

I walked the edge of my lot, facing inward, looking for other signs of house damage. The roof looked about the same. Too bad, I thought, I was hoping Sandy might have torn off the unsightly green roof moss that gave our house an organic, Middle Earth charm I can do without.

Same for the windows, siding and gutters. All where they should be. I guess we in our little lake community had once again come out ahead of the curve.

It took some time to realize just how bad it was, much longer to comprehend how much worse it would get.

Taking a second lap around the house, I turned around to inspect the borderlands and saw the first sign of real damage — a fat old pine in the corner of an adjacent lot had toppled into the driveway of my backyard neighbor's place. The pine, a good thirty feet tall and nearly half that wide at the base, had fallen just past the corner of his house.

My neighbor came out just as I made my way over, marveling at the round wheel of dirt in front of me where the pine's root system, some six feet in diameter, had torn out of the ground.

"Wow," I said to my neighbor, "you were lucky."

"Lucky?" he said, somewhat incredulously.

"That could have hit your house," I said. "And have you heard the reports about the Shore? I guess we were all pretty lucky around here. It could have been a lot worse."

"Yeah," my neighbor said. "But ..."

Then I saw what he was looking at. The pine had fallen on both of his cars. We pushed our way through the branches for a closer look. One car looked like it was just a little scratched up, the other had taken a direct hit from the trunk, its top crunched and most of the windows shattered.

"Well, I guess there's lucky, and there's lucky," I said, trying to sound less stupid and more sympathetic. "They can probably fix that. I bet they can fix that."

"Who do I call about this?" he asked. "My car insurance? Home insurance?"

"His insurance?" he asked, pointing to his pine-bearing neighbor's property.

I wasn't quite sure, which kind of surprised me. I'm a bit of a know-it-all and even when I don't know the answer, I usually have a convincing guess. Yet here I was, telling a guy with a new flat-top convertible how lucky he was, and I didn't have a clue about the insurance. It was almost as if I was in some kind of fog, but I didn't know why. If the radio reports were accurate, we were lucky. Trouble was, I didn't believe it, nor was I successful in convincing my poor neighbor of his good fortune.

Things felt, I don't know, *wrong*. I'm not one to put stock in premonitions, but right then and there, I got a really bad feeling and a complementary chill, perhaps from the tip of the iceberg we were standing on.

Obviously I didn't have the answers my neighbor required. I needed more information, and fast, so I excused myself, went back inside and planted myself in front of the Little Black Radio, which would become a supporting character in this extended journey into darkness.

We listened to the Little Black Radio in the kitchen while Lisa updated me on our emergency supplies. Daylight had broadened considerably, so I could see the smear of minute-steak grease that had drooled down a cabinet. What a mess.

What a mess down at the Jersey Shore as well. Governor Christie, assuming the militaristic take-charge cadence of New York Mayor Rudy Giuliani during the days following 9/11, was talking about the three phases of government response — preparation, rescue and recovery.

Some six to eight hours after the storm had subsided, we were still in the rescue phase. That wasn't good. They were still trying to get to people stuck on the barrier islands, and there was a lot of wreckage, gas leaks, buckled roads.

"There's a house on Route 35," Christie said.

We all tend to be provincial, and there's always some tension between New York and New Jersey. So of course we were more interested in reports from our Garden State. But you could not possibly ignore the news coming out of Long Island, the outer boroughs and even Manhattan.

Two of the reports stood out and drove home the nightmarish severity of our situation. They were still finding bodies on Staten Island, where the storm surge caught many by surprise and literally washed people out of their homes.

Then there was the news from Breezy Point, on the tip of the Rockaway Peninsula, where Queens kind of wraps around the southern tip of Brooklyn and flips a middle finger to Coney Island. The fire department, cut off by chest-high waters, could not control a blaze that eventually consumed more than 100 homes, including many owned by cops, firefighters and other first-responder heroes of the September 11 World Trade Center attacks.

Amazingly, no one died in the massive inferno, thanks largely to firefighters who took to boats to make rescues. Not so on Staten Island, the forgotten borough, where about two dozen fatalties eventually would be counted.

I was tempted to go back to my neighbor and argue the "lucky" point, but we all had more important matters to contend with. This was no ordinary storm, we realized, no matter what we were seeing from our yards.

We absorbed another press conference from the Little Black Radio — Christie's authoritative wheezing had been replaced by the nasal monotone of New York Mayor Bloomberg, whose consistently unflappable calm can be annoying at times but was oddly comforting now. Both elected leaders vowed that everything that could be done was in fact being done. Bloomberg was doing it in two languages.

But there were so many reports from so many places, how could they even know? I kept waiting for the top and the bottom of the hour, the points where WCBS generally gives you a quick wrap of the headlines. But there were too many, so they just kept tossing out the updates as they came in.

Rising to the surface of the information overload were the reports coming in from the power companies. Clearly, the majority of life-threatening emergencies were spread along the shores, where the storm surge added to the damage with exponential force. Sandy's victims, though, were everywhere. The wind had torn through North Jersey like a hair trimmer on a five-day beard. Blackout estimates region-wide claimed that almost everyone lost power at some point and that a good two-thirds of us were still off the grid, maybe more in Morris County.

"Limited restoration today," I heard one guy from Jersey Central Power & Light say. "We will begin restoring power tomorrow after we assess."

His announcement hardly was a surprise, but it did change our mindsets. We would not be able to measure the impact of this storm by comparing it to other storms, not even the hurricane that hit here just over a year ago. Irene was a naughty child. Sandy was her big sister, an immature, sociopathic teen who had just pitched a hissy upside our head.

So the hope of near normal by dinner segued into discussion of long-term issues. If power restoration was off the board for at least a day, we needed to reassess our assets. There was the battery shortage and our lack of a generator, fireplace or supplementary source of heat. There was our fully stocked fridge and an even fuller basement freezer, packed with expensive meats and other perishables we bought in bulk and on sale. *Ironically to save money*, I thought as I calculated some $400 worth of steaks, ribs and seafood and wondered how long before the inevitable thaw would defrost my food budget.

Heat was the more immediate concern. I pulled out my iPhone and *viola!*, I had my signal back. I immediately went to my trusty Weather Channel App and looked at the forecast. *Uh-oh*. A cold front was coming in and it would drop below freezing tonight, with colder temps right behind it.

So the freezer food was thawing out and we were going to freeze. Now, that's irony for you.

Still, we were clearly among the lucky ones, a phrase that would come to both comfort and annoy us in the coming days. We were in a bad situation, but we were alive, there was no major damage to our home and our neighborhood — what we could see of it — was intact. How do you compare that to loss of life or having your home washed out to sea?

Exactly.

We also accepted the grim realization that our neck of the woods wasn't a priority among emergency responders. They would get to us when they got to us. The JCP&L guy was now saying that most of us would have our power back in seven to ten days.

Seven to ten days. And it sounded like we would not be among the first. And someone had to be last. Seven to ten days.

"Complete restoration might take longer," the radio said.

There wasn't a whole lot we could do about it, so we smiled at each other and agreed patience and calm would be our allies. As the days went on, some would panic, some would give in to anger. Not us.

My wife, the patient one, smiled again, sat in the light of our living room picture window and opened her Kindle. I sat in my easy chair and stared at the blank TV. Last night was Monday. We had already missed recording some of our shows on the DVR. We hadn't yet watched the latest episode of "Boardwalk Empire." I was missing the plays of the week on ESPN.

I looked at the clock on my iPhone. Three minutes had passed since we agreed to be calm. Seven to ten days. Good Lord.

If this was the New Normal, I thought, then what we needed to do was establish a routine, ideally based on as much of our old routine as we could recreate now that we were .... *Amish*. It was morning, and it was breakfast time. What would we be doing under normal circumstances? Well, I would have the TV news on while I was reading or working online. OK, that did not fit into the New Normal paradigm.

Then it hit me, the short-term solution to our journey back to civilization — *coffee!* We hadn't had our morning coffee. No wonder I was in such a fog, talking stupid to the neighbors and staring at a TV that had no hope of entertaining me.

Surely there must be a way to make coffee. We can still boil water, pour it through the coffeemaker and there you go, Lisa said. *Brilliant girl.*

We got up and headed back to the kitchen. Maybe some eggs ... *yes!* And some toast ... *no!* Let's keep calm and not get ahead of ourselves, I thought. Let's make the coffee and work our way up from there.

Lisa boiled the water and I went to get the coffee beans ... *oh, crap.* We are coffee snobs who save lots of money by buying good beans and grinding them ourselves. We even have a backup grinder in case of emergencies, at least emergencies that don't involve a loss of electrical service.

Seven pounds of gourmet beans, a pot of boiling water and no way to turn them into coffee. I briefly considered panic, but it was still only twelve minutes since we vowed to keep a cool head.

But no TV? And no coffee? *Are you freaking kidding me?* I might not make it to lunch!

We improvised a breakfast out of some grapes and stale mini-muffins left over from the book-launch party four days earlier for my new novel, "The Puddingstone Well" (editor's note: insert product placement here). We had plenty of food and figured we might as well start with the elder perishables and eat our way forward.

After breakfast, I checked my mobile internet connection again and there was an intermittent signal. A quick check of the email inbox and I was off to Facebook, where many of my friends had shared their nervous anticipation just 24 hours earlier. There were the usual postings of music videos for "A Hard Rain's A Gonna Fall" and "Bad Moon Rising" and more leftovers from the Irene hit parade.

Many of the usual suspects had not yet checked in. I tried to do a mental inventory of friends with smart phones, figuring the lines were down for most desktop users. So far, there were status updates from my friends in Boonton, where the whole town was down, and from Randolph, another sprawling suburban township where the major roads were choked with trees and other obstructions.

On it went, from the anguish of Sussex County residents far more isolated than us to the crowded river-crossing cities on the Jersey side of the Hudson. The train stations in Jersey City and Hoboken were flooded and the tide was surging in their streets.

My friends to the south, in Somerset and Middlesex counties, had taken their lumps as well. It was a relief to hear that the Raritan, South Branch and Millstone rivers, which regularly spilled over their banks in battered boroughs such as Bound Brook and Manville, were surprisingly calm since very little rain fell. Sandy's full-moon tidal surge, however, came higher and swifter than anticipated, ravaging Raritan Bay towns in Middlesex such as Sayreville and Perth Amboy, where the revitalized waterfront had taken a direct hit.

Others — many others — expressed dread about their vacation houses on the Shore. Most of the barrier island towns, from Sea Bright to Long Beach Island, were closed to everyone except emergency responders. Even my friends in the newspaper business on Shore beats could do no more than line up and wait for the governor to wave the green flag.

It was frustrating to miss the 24-hour news coverage of the storm on television and the isolation quickly drove me batty. I was a local journalist by trade; when people wanted to know what was going on around town, around New Jersey, I was one of the people they counted on to tell them. At least until I was laid off last year, along with a lot of other journalists who were not covering Sandy, either.

I still had my network of Facebook and email friends, though, so I decided to take a ride and report for myself what kind of damage was keeping most of us in the figurative dark, at least until sundown, when figurative would become uncomfortably literal.

My lake community — some 160 homes — is built around a charming 12-acre lake no bigger than a pond, with two roads forming a circular beltway around the perimeter. I've circumnavigated the beltway after many a storm here for a quick status report on my entire neighborhood. The initial survey this morning was encouraging.

There were less than a dozen trees down and all roads were passable, although the police later closed a tight corner on the outer edges. A tree had partially toppled and was leaning on a power line, but everything seemed to be intact. Although I had been able to get through with my sedan, there wasn't enough room for a truck or even a large SUV to pass. The police of course had to block the corner and reroute traffic to a very handy detour road, so the blockade was no big deal.

Except that one line provided power to half the neighborhood — my half of the neighborhood — and what we didn't know at the time is that the blockade would remain, the tree would lean and the power from the line would not resume for the better part of two weeks.

Elsewhere in my Lake Intervale section, another tree had clipped the corner of one roof on the other side of the lake, and of course there was my neighbor's car. There was little or no other obvious damage. Only one other road was blocked by a tree and the fire department was already there sawing it up and dragging it out of the way. Yes, the fire department was armed with chainsaws and engaged in tree removal. A curious allocation of resources. Fire, it seemed, was not the primary concern at the moment.

Sure, there were branches and debris all over. And leaves, lots of leaves, since we were at the peak of autumn's arboreal molting. Messy, but no evidence that the mother of all superstorms — the one they were talking about on the radio — had paid us a visit.

Then I crossed the road into the next neighborhood, the next town, and a completely new world.

Less than a mile from my front door, I turned a corner into Mountain Lakes, a bedroom community that recently celebrated its centennial. Heavily wooded, about 4,000 people live there in distinctive and historic million-dollar homes on narrow roads that wind around half a dozen lakes.

Very few of those roads were passable now. Not only were there trees, poles and power lines down, but in many places, the trees, poles and lines were twisted into knots lying on front lawns, streets and fences. Even more astonishing, a lot of the poles had snapped clean in half. Same with the trees, although the worst damage seemed to come from ancient pines, like the one on my neighbor's car, that had uprooted and toppled from the base. Mountain Lakes was loaded with them … maybe not so much now as before.

It didn't look like storm damage. It looked like a tank squadron had plowed through the high-heeled borough, firing at random targets along the way. The destruction fell shy of complete, but there was surely enough to convince the residents of Mountain Lakes that they had lost the battle and were no longer in charge.

Some of the streets were so narrow, and so many of them were impassable, that I nearly ran out of detours in a town I've been driving through for 38 years. I had been careful about driving over fallen lines — hey, some of them could be live, right? — but I grew worried that might prove tricky if I had to make a K-turn. I remembered the many warnings I heard on the radio about not driving unless you had to. Maybe it was time to follow instructions and not cause a new problem for emergency personnel who probably had bigger fish to fry.

It took me nearly a half-hour to turn around and go home, even though I was never more than about two miles from my driveway. I eventually had to make a K-turn and try to retrace my route, but there were so many obstructions that I found myself on roads I didn't know existed. Trial and error finally released me from the maze and I happily headed back to my little quarter acre. I had seen enough for one day.

The rest of the day, like many of the days ahead, blurred for hours at a time. We sat, we read, we listened to the

Little Black Radio and marveled how well its batteries were holding up. We cooked some eggs and grilled my wife's tasty homemade bread into toast. It was a simple, satisfying meal befitting the simple existence we now shared.

We recalled the words of the JCP&L spokesman, who had said today was reserved for assessment and repairs would begin tomorrow, which really could not come soon enough. So we decided to turn in early once again. Sleep through the sea of darkness that had descended upon our safe, comfortable, illuminated lives and bring us that much closer to the light of a new day full of promise and possibility.

The urge to write, though, dogs me like a drug habit. Since my layoff from a job of writing and editing 16 months earlier, I had written and self-published two novels. And I had always enjoyed writing poems and verse whenever the inspiration struck. Certainly, Sandy was the kind of gal who might inspire many a story and poem, so before I turned off the lights — metaphorically speaking, of course — I pulled out my iPhone, logged on to Facebook and tried to share some of my day.

And it came out something like this, attached to a photo of my wife reading her Kindle by candlelight:

Kindle candle burning brightly
I miss my dose of cable nightly
One more shower, maybe two
Then water heater says it's through
Did Dante write of such a hell
As waiting for JCPL?
Brother spare me from your dime
I'll hit you up some other time
Unless you have what I don't got
Brother can you spare a kilowatt?

Deep meaningful thoughts, as you can see.
Hey, get off my back. It was a long day, all right?

DAY 3: Casual Wednesday, Part I

"We're gonna have a lot of work to do. I don't want anybody to feel that somehow this is all going to get cleaned up overnight. We want to make sure people have realistic expectations." — President Barak Obama, visiting Brigantine, New Jersey, Wednesday, October 31, 2012

Still sorting through the cornucopia of debris on our lawns, roads and shorelines, we were beginning to see the collateral damage spawned by Sandy's fury.

The governor declared his intention to cancel, or at least postpone, Halloween.

"I can't imagine that it's going to be safe for kids to go around for Halloween tomorrow," Christie said yesterday. "If conditions are not safe for trick or treating on Wednesday, I will sign an executive order ..."

And he actually did, rescheduling it for Monday. Nov. 5. Now, one might argue the validity of that order and surely under normal circumstances, Christie and New Jersey's feisty Democratic legislature would lock horns over over his legal right to manipulate holidays with at least some semblance of religious relevance.

But we were all trying to cooperate now, stay on the same page and share our long-term challenges, which chafed at the mindset of many New Jersey natives, who love to argue and generally pull out a big can of whup-ass for anyone who would interfere with their plans.

Remember when I wrote about things feeling wrong? This is the sort of thing I was talking about. People were getting along, offering to share supplies with neighbors, waving at power-company linemen as they drove by. People were driving slowly, carefully and politely.

This was not the New Jersey I knew. And before the end of the day, our governor, Chris Christie, the Republican Party's designated junkyard dog, and our incumbent Democratic president would be hugging on the Jersey Shore like Dons at a Godfather convention.

In the news business, we call this a "man bites dog" story. I'm not sure, my iPhone has a small screen, but I think I saw Christie nibbling on the president's ear during their embrace, which was long enough to be awkward.

Especially when Christie's cherished GOP candidate, Mitt Romney, was standing by, desperate for attention in some swing state he was destined to lose. In their joint press conference, Christie praised Obama like New York Jets Coach Rex Ryan was praising his underachieving quarterback, Mark Sanchez. Sanchez, along with our commander-in-chief, would come out of election week with his starting job intact.

Obama, returning the favor, praised Christie for his tireless, aggressive leadership and even quoted Christie's famous line during the Preparation phase for Hurricane Irene — "Get the hell off the beach."

Sadly, in many shore towns, there was no beach left to get the hell off of.

Still, it was good to have presidential feet on the ground in New Jersey, especially since some of those smug New Yorkers were miffed he was here and not there. Oh, those rivalries are strong, too strong to be pre-empted by a mere superstorm.

The president reported that more than 2,000 FEMA personnel had their feet on the ground as well and that he would not tolerate any delays or red tape.

"I've instituted a 15-minute rule, essentially on my team," he said. "You return everybody's phone calls in 15 minutes, whether it's the mayors, the governors, county

31

officials, if they need something, we figure out a way to say yes."

Meanwhile, Mitt Romney was out of state and out of mind. Granted, it was likely prudent that he kept the campaign circus outside of our blast zone. But you had to wonder if this was the moment where this pick 'em-odds presidential election would turn, with the president sounding presidential and offering his shoulder to victims while one of his loudest Republican critics proudly followed two respectful steps behind.

But I'm getting ahead of myself here. The president's visit occurred in the early afternoon and, as the New Normal took hold, it was a long morning. A new word — contingency — was trending on my street, which had become the server for our new neighborhood intranet. That's how information would spread in this neighborhood when I was a kid. The women would gather at the beach or a street-corner bus stop to dish and discuss while the men would do their business on the side of the road or in a driveway, often gathered around an open car hood. Smaller gatherings of neighbors, men and women alike, also would form spontaneous discussion groups right in the middle of our quiet streets.

In recent years, there were fewer face-to-face neighborhood discussions as people communicated more via email and social media, even with their next-door neighbors. Kids, too, followed the pattern since pickup ballgames in the street, on the beach or even a big yard were a rare event. These days, kids need uniforms, regulation fields, coaches and sanctioned referees to play a game.

We were now at a point where everybody was checking on everyone else. I'll admit it, I don't know the names of a lot of people in my neighborhood and rarely stop to chat with many of them. But by this morning, I was having my third post-storm conversation with the guy on my corner who I had spoken to exactly once in the ten or so years he's lived here. He, too, had ignored my existence up to this point, but was now eager to trade information.

This guy also was the first on my block to fire up a generator, another significant new element of the New Normal. I remember when my father used to admire the neighbors who could put a Cadillac in their driveway.

"And he gets a new one every two years," my Dad said of one man, as though that alone validated his success.

Now, the New-Normal status symbol of choice was a generator, and being among the have-nots, I felt the envy my Dad must have swallowed when our next-door neighbor was buffing a can of Turtle Wax into the hood of his new Sedan de Ville.

We weren't yet envious of the neighbors with working fireplaces. It was 64 degrees in the house when we got up. Heat was not yet the most immediate concern. We had gone two nights and were now in our third day with no power, no TV, no lights, none of the creature comforts we had been trained to take for granted.

The subject of staying warm, though, was making a move on the backstretch and catching up fast to the front of our cluttered minds. It had gotten colder — today's predicted high was in the 40s — and the thermometer was threatening a drop to the low 20s overnight.

The phrase "contingency plan" began to trend elsewhere, too. Sure, we may get our power back today — we had already set a new record for longest blackout — but we had to face the facts. It could be a week or longer before we got our power back, And at this rate, the house was going to get too cold to occupy.

If we had to evacuate — a concept I simply could not wrap my head around — where would we go, exactly? Of course we had friends and family who would be willing to take us in, but many of them were in the exact same dilemma as we were. Surely there was some place we could go, but identifying that destination meant we would have to create a contingency plan.

We started by considering our most obvious options, which in cases like this should include government help. We knew the governor and the president were personally helping to clean up the Shore properties, but what about us in Low Priority-ville? Surely there must be a local shelter. Maybe it was time to see what our municipal leaders were doing.

The good news was that my town of Parsippany had established a shelter before the storm, at Lake Hiawatha Elementary School.

The bad news was that of 14 public schools in Parsippany, the one building to sustain damage was Lake Hiawatha Elementary. *Oh, Sandy, you spiteful harlot.*

Fortunately, the shelter had been moved to the nearby Parsippany Community Center, a versatile facility I am much more familiar and comfortable with. The two-story building hosts a variety of municipal offices and public organizations, including the Women's Theater Company, where we are regulars at their productions in the downstairs Parsippany Playhouse. We decided to see what might be available for us there.

Upstairs, the center has offices, a billiards lounge, a huge kitchen and a substantial banquet room, along with some roomy bathrooms. It was a perfect place to establish a shelter and there were several municipal employees there to show us around and make us comfortable.

Once we signed in, we were directed to the kitchen, where coffee was brewing and a spread of bagels had been delivered from a local shop. The coffee was hot and the bagels were that-morning fresh (trust me, we know our bagels in New Jersey).

We took our breakfast to the banquet room, where various families and individuals had claimed one of many round tables available. Maybe a dozen tables were occupied, with three times that many waiting for more of Parsippany's tired, poor and huddled masses. Most were huddled close to the big-screen TV in the corner, which was tuned to the local ABC News affiliate in New York.

I looked at my watch. It was about 8 a.m. and ABC's "Good Morning, America" had been pre-empted for local news, which of course was 24/7 Sandy. This, two full days after the storm hit. I recall from my own viewing that extended news coverage began over the weekend and was round-the-clock beginning the morning before the first hints of Sandy's presence crossed into our lives. If Sandy were a TV series, she surely would be renewed for a second season.

We instinctively drew nearer to the TV. I realized it was not a true HD TV, but rather an old rear-screen projection unit. The image was less than state-of-the-art, but we were dying to see the video images of what we had only been able to hear and read about up to now.

Like the early radio reports, though, there was so much to show in both New York and New Jersey that they never stayed in any one place for very long. So all we got were the briefest of visual bites. And of course, there was little in the way of good news to brighten our morning. In fact, the pain of seeing the damage, especially to our beloved Jersey Shore, quickly became too much to process or bear.

The bagel proved far more satisfying, and we remembered they had nice, warm, clean bathrooms as well. We abandoned the TV and headed for the rest rooms to indulge in adjusted New Normal luxury.

We swapped stories and information with our fellow victims and quickly formed the kind of steely bond that often is forged in the heat of a crisis. We felt especially bad for the young kids, most of whom seemed too disoriented to act out. It was a quiet and diverse group, reflecting Parsippany's changing demographics — Middle Eastern and Asian families made up half the group, while the rest were a melting pot of couples and individuals who shared what little optimism they could muster.

One father told me he had a generator and a fireplace — I envied him immediately — but a tree had hit his house and it was not safe to stay there. So he and his four kids were sleeping at the shelter until he heard from the building inspectors and his insurance adjuster.

The shelter also offered its services as a charging station for our electronic and mobile devices, which became another essential emergency service around the state. I happily plugged my iPhone into an outlet strip and fed it some breakfast. After running my car to charge it twice on Tuesday, I was worried that my gas gauge had dropped below a quarter tank. I could only do that so much before running out of gas, which was becoming another serious concern.

Very few of the gas stations in New York and New Jersey had power and some of those that did could not get gas delivery because the delivery trucks were backed up at the few refineries and filling depots still in operation. Gasoline was the one liquid most of us forgot to stock up on and a panic was quickly building. Even coffee ranked a distant second to the prospect of a New Jersey driver being cut off from his gasoline supply. All those generators needed gas, too.

The ramifications of Sandy were beginning to stack like cordwood. Having finished breakfast and with a fully charged iPhone in hand, the day was still young and we had no idea what to do next.

I considered my short-and long-term future prospects and made an executive decision: I logged onto Facebook and invoked my limited authority to declare this a Casual Wednesday.

We took a different route home to see how other neighborhoods around town had fared. The most startling revelation was that almost all of the traffic signals in our well-trafficked town were not working. No wonder the mayor had declared a state of emergency and closed our roads to all but emergency traffic.

Good thing power had been cut to the red-light cameras as well. Some towns could have made a fortune mailing a ticket to virtually all of the cars on the road for violating the mayor's edict.

Then again, given the timely publishing of this book, some of those tickets may not yet have arrived. Power had been cut to the post offices as well, and the U.S. Postal Service, which recently announced a fiscal-year loss of about $16 billion, was in no hurry to deliver our junk mail and utility bills, nor were we in a hurry to receive them.

The only stretch of our main local highway, Route 46, that appeared to have power was a mile-long strip directly opposite our neighborhood. Talk about dumb luck — a new restaurant, Sonoma Chicken Coop, had just opened up along that strip and there was a line just to get in their parking lot. Some new manager was going to make his bonus figure this month. That line, however, was dwarfed by the line at the gas station down the road. The Shell Station on the corner of 46 and Cherry Hill Road was the only gas station we saw that was open and the line went up the highway, under a railroad trestle and literally into the next town.

It was yet another item of evidence submitted to define the New Normal. *First you get the gas, then you start the generator, then you get the power, then you get the women ...* sorry, I drifted into "Scarface" there for a minute, when "Mad Max" would have been a better choice for the on-point movie reference.

With nowhere good to go that didn't have a line, we drove home, bundled up, pulled out our readers and tried to relax with the little Black Radio offering commentary in the background. The next controversy was coming out of Staten Island, which was reeling from the astonishing tidal surge that lashed its shoreline and was still yielding bodies.

People in the most outer of the outer boroughs were up in arms about the New York Road Runner's Club, which was announcing its intention to run the New York Marathon on

37

Sunday morning as scheduled. And Mayor Bloomberg had their back. He was recalling how Rudy Giuliani earned effusive praise for making sure the race was run on schedule some six weeks after 9/11, partly to give New Yorker's a feel-good moment and partly to spit in the face of Al Qeada and declare we would not be moved.

Bloomberg, of course, was discounting the fact that the World Trade Center attacks did not compromise the infrastructure of the entire Tristate region, nor was it being run less than a week after the bombing, with tens of thousands of runners working their way through neighborhoods with no power, their safety and welfare assured by thousands of cops and volunteers who would surely be needed elsewhere.

It was ridiculous enough to be amusing, unless of course you were a resident of Staten Island or one of the evacuated zones in lower Manhattan, Brooklyn and Queens. Lives had been saved with that unprecedented evacuation, but some business owners and high-rise apartment residents were being told they might not get to move back in until Thanksgiving.

Later that afternoon, while we were trying to relax, I saw the son of a neighbor pull in to check on his mother's house. I knew he worked for the state as a full-time tree-removal crew member and I was naturally anxious to interrogate him on what he had seen.

"They had us out there Monday night," he said. "And I was never so scared in my entire life. Route 287 (our interstate freeway going north to upstate New York and south to the Shore points) south of Morristown was the worst I have ever seen in this job. There were trees in the middle of the highway, everywhere. Something, I don't know what, blew in and broke a window in my truck."

"I hope they are paying you overtime," was all I could say.

"To hell with overtime," he said. "I don't need it that bad."

Now I had heard everything, a state worker who lost interest in overtime pay. What had our little state come to in such a short amount of time? Black was white, up was down and now this. What next, the governor would declare odd-even gas rationing or something?

A few hours later, the sun was setting, the temperature was dropping and we were wondering what kind of night lay ahead. I took one more drive to see what, if any, progress had been made by the tree cutters and power-line workers, armies of which we were told had come from other states to straighten out our mangled power grid.

I hadn't seen many trucks on our earlier trip and I wasn't seeing any now. What I did notice was that the Wendy's on Route 46 had power, was open and, more importantly, it was not oppressively crowded inside, despite a long line at the drive-up window. Lisa and I had not discussed dinner and I figured bringing home a hot meal might be a nice surprise.

When I went inside, the fast-food joint had taken on a Starbucks vibe. Half the tables were taken up by people who were using their laptops while charging in whatever outlets they could find on the wall. Most of them had already cleared away their meal wrappings — if they indeed had even taken a meal here — and were sipping a coffee or soft drink. All that was missing was upholstered furniture and a hip music mix.

In fact, the restaurant was piping in Christmas music, which I noted with genuine amusement and shared with the nice middle-aged lady taking my order.

Another customer — a sixty-something woman dressed in Bohemian style, perfectly appropriate for a cold Casual Wednesday — had keyed in on the holiday mix and was not amused.

Looking shy but shaken — I sensed she was not comfortable with confrontation — her hands and voice shook as she asked the server if she understood "how inappropriate it is to be playing this music, people singing about winter wonderlands, and let it snow, for goodness sake, I'm just appalled that you would do that. Can't you turn the station to something else? This is so upsetting, I can't begin to tell you!"

The server tried to be sympathetic.

"It's not up to us what they play, it gets pumped in," she said. "If it was up to me, I would turn it off, but I don't even know how."

"Well, I would think that Wendy's wouldn't want to antagonize all these people," she said with a sweeping arm gesture to the 25 or 30 people in the dining area, none of whom appeared bothered in the least. "Well, I for one will never eat at another Wendy's ever again. You people should be ashamed of yourselves for being so insensitive. They're still finding dead bodies out there, you know."

She stormed off with a Sandy-level chip on her shoulder as I made silent eye contact with the server. She had laughed at my joke about the music just before the lady interrupted us.

I paused for effect, smiled and said, "See? Santa's going to be really angry with you."

"I feel bad," she said. "But what can I do?"

"Just stay cool," I replied. "If we sweat the small stuff like she is, we'll never survive this mess. You gotta keep your perspective."

I took my food and left, having comforted the server lady and gathered a hot meal for myself and my wife. But I had to ask myself how many more days before I was jumping ugly with strangers for little or no reason. How long before all of us were doing that? It was still only Day 3.

We ate our burgers by candlelight, read some more and turned in early for a third straight night. Once again, my urge to write struck and I pulled out my iPhone to share some words with friends:

Sandy why you got to blow so hard?
I've got trees uprooted in my yard
Seaside Park is in the sea
The levee breached in Moonachie
Sandy why you got to blow so hard?

Sandy leave the sand upon the shore
I don't really need it in my store
No use for extra wind, you see
Cause we got Guv'na Chris Christie
Sandy leave the sand upon the shore

Sandy if you really wouldn't mind
Blow that damn tree off my power line
Freezing cold sooner than later
Cause I ain't got no generator
Sandy if you really wouldn't mind

Sandy you done gone and done me wrong
I ain't had no TV for so long
You and I we need to talk
Don't want you blowin' down my block
Sandy you done gone and done me wrong

This is pretty good stuff, I thought. *When this is over, I really ought to write a book.*

DAY 4: Fried Lasagna

"I have 2.4 million people out of power. I've got devastation on the Shore. I've got floods in the northern part of my state. If you think right now I give a damn about presidential politics, you don't know me." — Gov. Chris Christie on Fox News, responding to inquiries about whether he would be available to help Mitt Romney tour storm damage in New Jersey, Thursday, November 1, 2012

It was becoming a numbers game.

The news writers and radio anchors had fallen into a rhythm of measuring our predicament by the number of electric-utility customers who were without power. As of this Thursday morning, more than 1.5 million New Jersey customers (referring to businesses and households, not individuals, so the number of affected individuals would be considerably higher) were without power in New Jersey, nearly as many in New York City and Long Island, where the recovery was taking longer than elsewhere.

Pennsylvania was not completely spared, with more than 500,000 customers still in the dark, mostly along the New Jersey border from as far south as Philly all the way up to Bucks County. The Keystone State victims included my stepdaughter and her husband, who were nervously hunkered down in the 100-year-old house they had just bought in Bangor a few months earlier. They were learning about the downside of home ownership in a hurry.

Didn't forget about you, Connecticut. There were more than 300,000 Nutmeggers rubbing sticks and stones for fire and warmth.

New Jersey started out with about 2.7 million customers cut off from their precious juice, so there was measurable progress being made as we entered our third day of recovery. But as the first responders progressed from repairs to substations and other major power intersections, bringing big chunks of customers back online, the numbers were dropping at a lower rate. And by the time they got to places like Mountain Lakes, it would take a lot of man hours just to bring single sections, blocks and even individual properties back up.

Many of us learned you could also track these numbers online, providing me with an activity that quickly progressed to stalker-level obsession. Jersey Central Power & Light, or JCP&L, as we wrote on our monthly checks, was responsible for nearly a million of those power-deprived customers. Public Service Electric & Gas — PSE&G to its buds — covered most of the rest, with Orange & Rockland covering some folks up top and Atlantic City Electric hooking up with a few more down low.

The JCP&L site, which was updated every 15 minutes, also broke down the numbers by county and municipality. So obsessors such as myself could watch their local numbers go down — or back up, as was often the case — and compare the progress to that of neighboring towns and counties. Place the numbers over a mental map and you could chart paths of progress, and almost visualize the line workers working their way towards or away from you.

Make a game of it. Turn it into an app and it might outsell Angry Birds, around here, anyway.

Numbers also were used to describe a response effort that included thousands of tree and power-line workers from out of state who had come to put our Humpty Dumpty state back together. JCP&L alone claimed to have as many as 14,000 people working on lines, poles, trees and other relief efforts, most of whom came from outside the state, from as far as Alabama, Texas and even British Columbia. PSE&G, of course, had their own skilled mercenary army as did the Long Island Power Authority, or LIPA, which was trying in vain to restore Queens, Brooklyn and the Long Island counties of Nassau and Suffolk. Those rich folk in the Hamptons might have to burn their period furniture before this episode was over.

Many people were getting understandably impatient after three nights in the dark and no real information about how much longer it would be for them. I was not a happy camper, either, but all it took was one trip to Mountain Lakes and I just knew this was something you could not possibly prepare for, and all we could do now was prepare for the long haul.

So we were still trying to remain calm and continue our watchful waiting, as they say in the medical field when they really don't know what else to do. But there were other numbers conspiring against us. One was on our thermostat, which plummeted overnight to a brisk 56 degrees in the morning. The five-day forecast contained similar numbers, highs in the 40s and lows in the 30s.

That meant we were headed for some three dog nights. See, there's another number for you.

Oh, and the long-range forecast included a nor'easter for early next week that would bring high winds, rain and possibly even snow. It wasn't just Sandy now. Mother Nature had joined in on the fun and was fixing to really mess with our heads.

My wife and I tried to crunch the numbers into the contingency plan we had yet to really embrace. Lisa's sister had her power back in Easton, Pa., just over the Delaware and a long hour from our address.

What's more, she had room in her freezer for our extensive inventory of perishables. Still somewhat in denial, however, we resisted the obvious need to examine such unlikely scenarios. They would get the power back on before the house got too cold to bear, before our freezer food started to thaw … before the nor'easter.

Right?

The subject of our freezer had come up several times already. Even before both of us lost our jobs, we both loved to eat, we both loved to cook and we never had an abundance of disposable income. Our solution was to stock up on good food at sale prices and store it in our big basement freezer or our makeshift garage pantry.

The freezer currently was at full capacity due in part to an extended depression in baby back rib prices at Costco. The Rib King (that would be me) knows this and recently had purchased three vacuum-sealed packages of three racks each.

We also had beef filets, an assortment of chicken, seafood and a tempting collection of Omaha Steak goodies, a gift from my sister, who knows the way to my heart is through my stomach. Oh, and my prize collection of Haagen Daz, which I curate like a sommelier fusses over wine. Without Haagen Daz and french fries, I would be half the man I am today.

If you know what I mean.

So our freezer represented more than mere provisions. It was the equivalent of our farm. Starving or not, no one wants to see their crops lost to a storm. It's just that in this case, my crops were chicken tenders, jumbo shrimp and half-price Toaster Strudels.

Oh yeah, and we had a couple of rolls of Taylor Ham, which means very little to readers outside Sandy's influence but slices to the heart of us here in New Jersey. The insiders know of what I speak. All the outsiders really need to know is that Taylor Ham is processed to the point that it can take care of itself in a tight spot.

So we focused our concern on the jumbo shrimp and the assorted super-premium frozen dairy treats that would be the first to go.

Experts on the radio offered useful numbers to their unusually captive audience, most of whom were in the same sinking ship as us. Refrigerator perishables, they said, were good for about 48 hours. Your freezer? Two to three days. Of course these estimates rightly err on the side of caution, but don't take in the nature of perishables. Ground beef, for example, spoils faster than, say, Velveeta.

Or Taylor Ham.

So *pshaw*, we said to the expert estimates. Our white goods would keep most of our stuff for at least twice that long, we estimated, based on the items in our fridge that were still nice and cold. We would not even open the freezer, we decided, until tomorrow, a full four days after the blackout began.

Here is where the genesis of our contingency plan took place. We would check the freezer tomorrow and, depending on the temperature inside, and the temperature in our split level, we would schedule our evacuation accordingly. If the freezer food was beginning to thaw, then staying would cost us real money, so we would pack it up and head for Easton. And with the power still out in Parsippany, why come back? Logic dictated a timely evacuation.

My mind bows to logic, but does not always follow. I immediately regressed to the thought that the blackout couldn't possibly last another day, could it? But the reports offered no evidence of support. Doubt and cold finally triumphed over my lack of imagination and I had to admit that evacuation was the sensible move.

Except for one thing — I was determined not to let anyone or anything remove me from my house. And no one would get me to leave, not without a tranquilizer dart and a crowbar, anyway.

I am one stubborn son of a bitch. You want to get me out of my house, the home that my family has owned for fifty years? *Bring it*, Sandy. I'll be waiting.

I kept this to myself for now, but Lisa knew. And kept it to herself.

We resumed our day, teetering between commitment to our sensible contingency plan and the baseless hope that our power would return before we were forced to fish or cut bait.

We continued to temper our fear with the omnipresent perspective that we were still counted among the lucky. But it wasn't getting any easier, especially when we learned that half our neighborhood had their power restored the night before. Those folks had won the Wednesday lottery, but they were an anomalous island in dark waters. I could not plot the source of their power, nor were there many linemen in our area, so there was no reason to believe that we would be next.

Meanwhile, local news sites and radio were slowly working regular news back into the mix, although much of it seemed to find its way back to Sandy.

The hottest topic was the New York Marathon and the folks on Staten Island were livid. With so many dead, so many homes gone and no power to speak of, the opposition was loud and angry. Residents were wondering about the fleet of generators that would be brought in to power the race's starting line at the Verrazano Bridge. Surely if those generators were on the island they could be put to better use. Then there were the truckloads of bottled water for the runners, another currently precious commodity in all the boroughs they would be running through.

Race organizers and Mayor Bloomberg vowed that no essential resources would be diverted from rescue and recovery to stage the race, but neither could explain how that could possibly be the case. What about the volunteers on the route who might not want to leave their powerless homes to hand out drinks on some powerless street cluttered with storm debris? And what about the cops who would be needed on every corner to keep the peace, and the emergency medical crews who would have to be on standby? If by some miracle these first responders weren't needed to help storm victims, shouldn't they be catching up on their rest?

By Friday, the controversy would conclude as Bloomberg and the club caved into public pressure and cancelled the race. One tipping point came when some hotel owners who had taken in storm victims refused to evict them for the runners from out of town. Of course, they waited until the last minute, so there were some grumpy Europeans and Africans who criticized the organizers for costing them thousands in travel expenses to a destination where they no longer had a place to stay.

The marathon controversy could have been avoided, of course, but it also was a case in point illustrating how many of us were wavering on important decisions because we simply could not believe the situation we were in, and refused to accept that it could last as long as the power companies were admitting with equal reluctance. We were all off our game, including Mayor Bloomberg, who could usually be counted on to make unpopular decisions if good sense dictated he do so.

Bloomberg still was doing his job in two languages and now, we were told, with sign-language interpretation by a woman who was signing at his press conferences with enough stylish flair that she earned her own fan club. Her silent choreography would eventually be lampooned on "Saturday Night Live," which also had some fun with Bloomberg and Christie. Certainly, by Saturday, we all would need a reason to laugh.

Too bad many of us would have to wait to see it because our power, and good humor, would still be missing in action when it aired.

We also doubted the likelihood that we would get to see the live benefit concert being planned for Friday night on NBC, headlined, of course, by New Jersey's Poet Laureate of the Jersey Shore, Bruce Springsteen. The concert also would feature Bon Jovi, who I once saw in a Jersey Shore club I am pretty sure had been lost to Sandy.

I began to wonder about other trivial matters. Our DVR was programmed to record our favorite shows but we obviously had missed many of them. At least the World Series was over and my Yankees had been eliminated some time ago. You cannot possibly imagine the anger I would experience if the Yankees had gone to a Game 7 World Series final during the blackout, leaving me with no choice but to listen to it on the radio and experience the historic moment through the failing eyes and curious vocabulary of Yankee announcer John Sterling.

We were longing for many of our creature comforts — TV, a fully functional kitchen, hot water ... more TV. Hey, what about my Sunday football? I'm a Giants fan and Big Blue was playing on Sunday. Surely we would have power back by Sunday.

Right? *Right?*

As the sun went down, my mind finally began to embrace the darkness. We were screwed, we were lucky, we were going to have to improvise for a while.

We would have to move beyond Casual Wednesday and explore a new level of casual, possibly bordering on primal. The high waters of the New Normal had risen above our heads and life as we knew it had been put in the corner for a time out.

Dinner was the next case in point. It was time to consume the more perishable of the perishables, beginning with the leftover lasagna. There was more than enough for two hearty dinners and it was time to use it or lose it.

Leftover lasagna is tailor-made for the oven or microwave, both of which had been taken offline. Our only functional cooking method was the stove, which we could still light with a match. That left three options for the leftover lasagna — boiling, grilling or frying. We chose frying and it proved to be a successfully tasty option.

Full of belly and cooling rapidly, we headed straight for bed, where another numbers game was adding up. We added another blanket to the bed, raising the total to four. Add the three layers of clothing I was wearing and, spooning with the missus, we were able to flip the bird to Sandy for one more night.

But before the metaphorical dousing of the night lights, I returned to Facebook one more time and fed my writing habit, offering these lessons learned from Sandy:

1. Even though people are freaking about no gas, the lines for drive-through restaurants are nearly as long as the gas stations. Amazing that our species can survive these storms in the first place.

2. I never liked camping and I never will.

3. If your oven doesn't work, it is possible to fry lasagna.

4. I miss TV so much I would even be willing to watch Nancy Grace at this point. I mean if she's the only thing on. And she doesn't dance ... or speak.

Like I said, the lights were gone, and the dark thoughts were taking over.

DAY 5: Crank Up the Tunes

"Keep in mind you got Bon Jovi and Bruce Springsteen, both supported the president ... where are the conservative performers? ... Is it a hurricane benefit or a concert for Obama?" — Fox News Analysts discussing the NBC Superstorm Sandy telethon, November 2, 2012

While marathoners and conservative talk show hosts debated the fairness of Superstorm Sandy's impact on their agendas, we victims, lucky and otherwise, played the hands we were dealt.

A new class structure had evolved. Those with power were, well, *in* power, with the generator-owners sitting pretty in second place.

Homes with fireplaces, too, were looked upon with jealousy by us green-eyed monsters on the bottom rung, with no power, heat or proper means to reheat lasagna.

My block and my powerless side of the neighborhood was divided roughly in three — Generators, Fire-makers and See-you-laters. I was one of just two heat-deprived home owners left on our block. The rest had fled for higher or hotter ground. *See you later*, they said, leaving me their numbers to call when someone got to the switch.

One of my neighbors, an older gentleman who was used to camping and braving the elements, lived in a home equipped with a fireplace but had not yet fired it up.

"I haven't used it in years and I would have to clean it first," he said, as though he had more important things to do, probably related to his retirement some 15 years ago.

"Come on, Rufus," I said. "What are you waiting for?"

Rufus, not his real name, as you probably figured out already, was old-school, so I tried, for the sake of his wife, to shame him into some chimney sweeping.

"Geez, Rufus, even a cave man knows he has to keep his women warm," I said.

Don't know if that grumble I heard was a tacit agreement or what, but two hours later, I could see smoke coming from that chimney. Rufus and his wife were sitting pretty. My work was done. Except it occurred to me that my wife was still cold. The thermostat had dropped like the Greek stock market last night and we woke to 52 lousy degrees. And the nor'easter forecast was gaining grimmity.

I made that up, *grimmity*. The New Normal required some new descriptive nouns, so I took the liberty under these grim circumstances.

So where were we? We were at 52 degrees on this sunny morning, Day 5 of our journey into failing self-sufficiency. We headed to the community center shelter, signed in and saw some familiar faces from our last few visits. We exchanged some hellos and some awkward conversation with a few new visitors to the shelter.

One, an elderly woman, was ranting about how she needed helping clearing the leaves from her yard. Like the lady at Wendy's a few days earlier, her badgering reminded me that we needed to keep some perspective here. My lawn maintenance had fallen behind schedule as well. So be it. Live to blow another day, that was the wisdom near the top of my current philosophy list.

I was sympathetic with another man, probably in his 60s and looking physically distressed. He mentioned a shortage of meds and his need for caffeine to help them kick in. I offered to draw him a cup of coffee from the community urn but he already had his. He obviously was starved for conversation as well, so I grabbed a cup of Joe for myself and lent him an ear.

He was a nice man, but either the meds were failing or the caffeine was failing in its catalytic role. Turned out he was a conspiracy theorist, too, either over- or under-caffeinated, or possibly both.

I listened to a few of his rather original plots against mankind until he launched into a harangue about how secret government cloud-seeding in the Sixties had corrupted our weather and was resulting in storms like Sandy and the similar tempests that were sure to follow.

This rant was hitting a little too close to home and seemed to be disturbing a few other people in the room, including the lady with the leaf-collection issue.

"Well, that's kind of an extreme theory," I said. "There's a lot of things out there affecting the weather, including random patterns."

"Maybe so," he said. "Just one man's opinion. Just because you don't agree don't mean it's not true."

Touche, my unstable friend. Just like we underestimated Sandy, I may have underestimated you. And hell, I kind of liked the idea of blaming the government for this mess we were in.

Then we all shared some breakfast, the shelter having received several buffet trays of fresh-cooked food. The hot breakfast entrees were donated from some nearby executive business breakfast conference that nobody showed up for. Go figure. And pass the syrup.

Our increasingly diverse support group of victims at the shelter was able to bond over pancakes and something we here in New Jersey can all share and be proud of: Taylor Ham. When the world is crumbling beneath your feet, you find common ground where you can.

Before we left, I made sure to give my iPhone a full charge. Between my frequent reconnaissance drives around town to search for linemen and the hours of idling my car for supplementary charges, I was running precariously low on gas. My very smart Lexus has a digital readout of the range of miles I have left in my tank, and it was nagging me like my eighth-grade math teacher. I was down to 70, 60 and now 48 miles. That might not even get us to Easton.

Don't ignore the numbers, my eighth-grade teacher, Mrs. Lexus (again, not her real name), used to say. *Pay attention to the numbers or you'll end up a day late and a dollar short.* And she was right. It was a numbers game now.

Speaking of nagging, my wife is very good about not doing that, despite all the reasons I give her to do so. One of the few things she is fond of nagging about, ironically, is keeping your gas tank filled. And she proudly claims she has never let the tank in her Ford Focus drop below a quarter-tank.

Hey, we have more gas than I realized, I thought as I asked for her keys.

I started up her car and gazed at her gas gauge, patiently giving it ample opportunity to reach its full measure, and … it stopped … just a hair above …. a quarter tank. *Geez, give a guy a break, would ya?* At this point, every small victory was a crowning achievement, every minor setback a crushing defeat. Put our lives under a microscope at this juncture and you would see the most innocuous actions magnified beyond reason. We were rushing in and out doors to preserve heat, pulling back curtains to let more sunlight and radiant heat inside, scolding each other when we left a flashlight on a moment too long. Every drop of gas, every minute of battery life, every British Thermal Unit counted at this point.

We just weren't very good at this, or at least I wasn't. I recalled Cub Scouts as a happy childhood activity, a merry band of brothers having fun with no real demands being made of us. But when I graduated to Boy Scouts, we were tasked with actual serious study, including frequent lessons on coping with the great outdoors and the dangerous elements found therein.

They were big on actual life experience, too, and I reached a crossroads when I was briefed on the Klondike Derby.

"Let me get this straight. We are going to camp outside. In the winter?" I asked my troop leader.

"Yeah, it'll be fun!"

"It'll be what now?"

"Fun!"

"What if it rains? What if it snows?"

"That's part of the experience. You'll see. We have a bunch of great activities. You'll love it."

"Not me, uh-uh."

"What do you mean? We're all going."

"Not me. No sir."

"All the Scouts do it."

"Well, then, I guess I'm not a Scout anymore."

And I never looked back. Easiest decision of my life. To this day, my idea of camping is staying in a hotel that doesn't have an indoor pool. I made sure selling her camper was in the prenup agreement I presented to the woman who foolishly became my wife.

Hey, I like my creature comforts. My wife, who grew up on a farm, sometimes says she was born a hundred years too late. Not me. If I had my druthers, I'd be flying a hovercar to my day job at Spacely's Sprockets.

I admit it. I'm soft. Soft and cuddly.

The sun managed to raise the temperature in the house to the mid-50s, so we sat down and tried it out, bundling up while we read and listening to the latest on the radio. Odd-even gas rationing: tomorrow. Gas lines: ridiculously long, even at some stations where there was no gas, only rumors that there would be. Springsteen TV telethon: on. TV and cable: off. Marathon: on, then off.

Utility updates: progressing slowly. If the outage numbers were a lottery, the pot was rolling over. There were still about a million and a half customers without power, including close to a million in New Jersey. In fact, while a few people had been restored, many more who had previously been restored had fallen back off the grid.

We absorbed a few more body blows from the radio and turned to our one scheduled task for the day. After four full days without power, it was time to check our freezer. We approached the task with nervous reluctance, my usual obsessive need to know tempered by the realization that what we discovered might force our hand and force us from our home, from our state and into a complete state of helplessness (no disrespect intended, Pennsylvania).

Good news and bad news. To our delight, our freezer had defied the odds and held its ice. Virtually everything had stayed rock-hard. Even the thick coating of frost on the shelves was still largely intact.

"See?" I said to Lisa. "Aren't you glad you didn't nag me about defrosting the freezer?"

If it was this good after four days, it should be good for at least a few more. We agreed to keep it shut and check it again on Sunday.

Now for the updated bad news: Our freezer may last until Sunday, but we might not. The sun was going down, as it had been doing with annoying regularity, and the temperature in the house was going down already. Surely by morning we would be in the 40s. Even if I could take it, I had to consider Lisa. She was as determined to stay by my side as I was to stay in my house.

Lucky, lucky, lucky. We were the lucky ones, I know …

I saved the day with a sudden epiphany. Among our rather impressive collection of antique musical instruments was a Victrola, actually a Sonora-brand wind-up phonograph player that is often mistaken for a Victrola. A Sonora, even by another name, doesn't need electricity. It runs on good old-fashioned elbow grease.

Sure, I had plenty of music in my iPhone, but I've always hated earbuds and music, in my mind, is meant to fill the air where everyone can share it. I also had a good selection of 78 rpm records to choose from in my library of more than 7,000 records (an obsession we'll discuss another day).

Delighted as the day we bought it, I cranked it up and spun some Benny Goodman. I beckoned my wife to come dance with me, but she was too cold and wanted to stay under her comforter. When I switched to Sinatra, however, she couldn't resist and, for a few sweet moments as the sun set in our living room, we waltzed our way to a warmer time and place, far from the shivering reality of our New Normal universe.

DAY 6: Putting Out Fire with Gasoline

"I've had to pee for two hours. Is this line even moving?" —
Woman sitting some 40 cars behind in a line for gas, Denville,
New Jersey, Saturday, November 3, 2012

We were going to bed earlier and earlier, hoping to
replace as many dark hours as possible with dreams of sunny
skies and short-sleeve comfort.

Quite naturally, we were waking up earlier, in the dark
and — on this Saturday morning — to 48-degree temperatures
in our sensibly mortgaged, split-level icebox. In fact, we woke
up in the middle of the night to discover a curious
phenomenon. As I attempted to roll over, pulling the blankets
over my exposed shoulder, I felt something odd between our
heads.

I switched on the little battery lantern and found our
king-size sheet bundled into a ball, like an extra head had
joined us for some bedtime game. Somehow we had yanked
the sheet out from under four heavy blankets. I could only
assume we were both to blame, probably grabbing that sheet
over and over to pull the blankets as high as they would go.

It defied the laws of physics, much as those magicians
do when they snap a tablecloth out from under a full dinner
setting. We would have to keep a watchful eye for other novel
phenomena wrought by the New Normal.

It was maybe 4:30 a.m. now and going back to sleep felt
like a remote possibility. I thought about passing the time
reading but my Kindle battery meter had already turned red.
Maybe it was time to go back to the car, charge up the phone
and take advantage of the toasty-bun seat warmers.

Mmm, toasty buns. I was hungry, too. The gas station down the road was not pumping gas, but the mini Dunkin' Donuts there was operating on generator power. Man, I haven't gone on a doughnut run this late at night since college, I thought. Maybe it was time to bring some nostalgia into the New Normal.

Then I got a better idea. The gas shortage — both in New Jersey and in my driveway — was now a serious problem. I had wasted some gas only yesterday looking around for a fill-up and the few stations open were jammed up like they were giving the gas away.

Gas also was trending on social media and my Facebook gang — about 270 friends if you are keeping score — was passing along tips about who was pumping where. The problem was that other people were doing this as well and as soon as a station took a delivery, and Facebook operatives sounded the alarm, cars gathered at the stations like ants at a picnic. Four-wheel flash mobs were forcing the overworked police to step in and keep the peace while hundreds of cars lined up, many with a trunkload of gas canisters to sate their hungry generators.

I checked Facebook and there were no current gas alerts so I decided simply to hit the highway and see what I could find. That had been the other popular tip for gas-hunters: The earlybird gets the fossil fuel.

Heading out to the car, I looked up and was compelled to pause. With no lights from the homes, no lights from the street and no clouds in the sky, the stars were as brilliant as I could ever remember seeing them anywhere. It was a brief but magnificent moment of unexpected inspiration. I'm a product of the suburbs and I rarely stray very far from the ambient light of civilization. I had seen some amazing skies in the Bahamas, where my sister taught school on a resident island, far from the glare of tropical resorts. But for this one moment, that throat-lumping panorama was hovering over my home base.

The sky was so very black, and the stars so burning white, I wondered how they could exist together. You could almost feel the heat radiating from the stars.

Almost. I could definitely feel the cold. It was in the 20s out there. I gazed at the sky for a little while longer until the siren's song of the seat-warmers lured me inside my Lexus. It was 5 a.m. and time to do the earlybird mambo.

I drove down the main road out of my neighborhood, slowly and carefully. There were some leaning trees and low wires, I remembered from my daytime patrols, and there were no streetlights to help you see your way. Another thing you had to look out for were the piles of cut-up trees spilling over into the streets. They were everywhere, and if you clipped one of those trunk-hunks with a wheel, you might find yourself walking home.

When I reached the highway, it was equally dark. It was eerie to drive through major intersections without the stoplights that so often annoy us but surely benefit us more than we give them credit for. Even faced with the rare freedom born of their absence, it was wise to slow down or even stop at the lights to make sure some other driver was not about to test his own newfound autonomy.

A few minutes later, I saw some police lights flashing a short distance from the turnoff to downtown Denville. I knew there was an Exxon station in the vicinity, so I turned and drove toward the light. Sure enough, there were police there, chaperoning a line of cars that had formed outside the station and down a long residential side street. It was pushing 5:30 and one of the patrolmen told me they were opening at six. I got on the line, counting only fifteen cars ahead of me. *Sweet.*

More cars quickly fell in behind me and suddenly, at 5:45, the line began to move. The police were not comfortable with the line extending into a residential neighborhood, so they directed us past the gas station and into an adjacent Walgreen's parking lot. Not a bad idea, I thought. The only other option would have been a single line of cars cutting straight through the downtown business district.

The pump jockeys were working fast but before I got out of the Walgreen's lot and into the station, I could see how the cops were improvising a manageable system to control the chaos. They directed the cars around the perimeter of the parking lot and lined them up in tight rows facing the exit. When it was one row's turn to enter the station, more cars would take their place while the next row, and the next, would file through the station and be refreshed by the latest cars to arrive.

It was a fairly complex system and it required several cops to execute, but it worked. As I finally got to the pump, I thought about rushing home with one full tank and coming back with the empty in my wife's Ford Focus.

Am I a good husband or what? If I played my cards right, I might even get to count this as a Christmas gift.

By 6:20, I had my gas and pulled out of the station, pointing at the surprisingly cheery pump jockey and shouting, "Who the man? You the man!" Then, in my best Schwarzenegger accent, I vowed that "I'll be back."

I went home, kissed the wife, grabbed her keys and was back at the station by 6:45.

Only this time, I was not at the front of the line. I had been directed to a row somewhere in the middle of the lot, and they were currently moving the lines to the left of me. That meant I would also have to wait for all dozen or so lines to the left and right to move before I did.

I got out of the car and evaluated my position. I was surrounded. We were packed like sardines. It would be a good two or three hours before I got to the front of this staggered line, and I couldn't get out of there now if I wanted to. I wasn't between a rock and a hard place. I was between a Volvo and a Toyota. Same difference.

I remembered to grab my charger so I could juice up the iPhone while I waited. With the heat at full blast, I was comfortable enough and took the opportunity to check the morning numbers online. The biggest number was that an estimated third of the Tristate area was still without power, representing many millions of homes and businesses, including more than 80 percent of gas stations.

More numbers were bandied about the line as people left their cars for cigarettes, stretching and pickup conversation. One man claimed to hear the station in front of us had received 8,000 gallons. At 20 gallons per customer — the official maximum per vehicle, including canisters — that meant there was enough gas for about 400 cars. Probably enough for those of us in the middle of the lot, we figured, but maybe not for the people still pulling in.

Returning to the car, it occurred to me that I was wasting gas by keeping the car running when it was very warm already and I wasn't going to move for at least another hour. I shut it off and went back to reading the morning papers on my iPhone. After about a half-hour, the car cooled off, so I went to start it up again and .... *Click, click, clickety-click*. Great. The battery was stone cold dead.

OK, daytime running lights, heater at full blast, radio on and I'm charging my iPhone. *Duh*.

By a small but significant stroke of luck, there were jumper cables in the back of my wife's Focus because her car had broken down just a few weeks ago when her alternator belt went, resulting in a similar dead battery.

I banged on the window of the Volvo, whose owner I had chatted with outside for a few minutes. He agreed to give me a jump, except he could not get his bent hood open. Nor could he lock it after popping the latch. *Sorry, dude, wish I could help you with that but I've got my own problems.*

I had one more option, a young woman sitting in the Toyota to my right. Her head was buried in a book and she was startled when I knocked on her window, staring down at her from my six-foot-two-inch wide frame, five-day growth of beard and the kind of bad hair day that would drive a teenager into therapy for years.

"Excuse me, miss, my battery died and you're the only one close enough to jump me. Can you help me out?"

She eyed me nervously, using her peripheral vision to triangulate the current location of the traffic cops. There were two nearby so she regained her calm and agreed to help me.

"Only thing is I don't know how to jump a car."

"Relax, all you need to do is pop your hood."

She did so quickly, clearly happy to have a valid excuse not to leave the car, even with the cops present at point-blank range. I maneuvered the clips into position, fired up the Focus and returned the hoods to their standard positions. Another crisis averted, it was on to the next unexpected challenge. Sitting there for so long, then standing outside the young woman's window, I caught a whiff of her cigarette. To my astonishment, it smelled good.

Mind you, I quit smoking in 1986, or about 40 pounds ago if you care to employ another unit of measure. And for the last 20 years or so, my rare cravings had vaporized in the wake of my growing hatred of second-hand smoke. I tolerated my wife's smoking because she tolerates, well, *me*, but until this near-frozen moment in time, I could not even remember how I ever appreciated the aroma and full, rich flavor of Marlboro Country.

I now regretted the decision to pass by the local Dunkin' Donuts on my way to the station. Doughnuts solve so many of life's little problems, including cigarette cravings.

And yes, that's right, Dunkin', you are free to spell your proper name as you choose, but I will spell doughnut correctly until you pry this dictionary from my cold, dead hands.

I fought the nicotine urge until my row was finally released from its fixed position and pointed at the gas station, where the fumes of precious petrol drove the intoxicating scent of processed tobacco back into my sordid past.

Giddy from solving my latest problem, I couldn't resist the urge to joke with the pump jockey, the same guy who filled my Lexus about three hours earlier. When he recognized me and welcomed me back, I replied, "I don't need any more gas, I just forgot to ask for directions."

Back home and full of gas — insert your punch line here — we settled in the living room, positioned ourselves in the sun and tried to keep warm while we passed some time with reading and radio reports. It was time for another Governor Christie's press conference, which were becoming prime-time entertainment in the New Normal. He was grinding through the details of his odd-even gas rationing order, which took effect at noon. In our storm-battered state, we had officially regressed to the 1978 energy crisis. Too bad the price of gas had not returned to 1978 levels, when you could buy two gallons of leaded regular for a little more than a buck.

Rationing, the governor assured us, would help ease the gas crisis and discourage old retired men with nothing better to do than clog those lines to top off the tank in their Oldsmobile. The idea was that people whose license plates ended with an odd number (or the last number on the plate) would gas up on alternate days — today, as of noon, it was an odd day, the governor explained, and that anyone with an even plate would be sent home.

"Tomorrow we will send the odd people home," he said, adding with a chuckle, "Wait, that doesn't sound right."

The wife, of course, was proud of her man's successful morning of hunting and gathering, which included bringing home hot coffee and McGriddle sandwiches from McDonald's for breakfast. I prefer the classic Egg McMuffin but the McGriddles were on sale, while we had already learned of Mickey D's curious policy of charging one dollar for any size coffee.

"What size would you like?" the counter lady asked.

"Um, large," I replied, wondering if it was a trick question, supremely confident in the knowledge that I had chosen wisely.

Remember, in the New Normal, every tiny victory was magnified into a crowning achievement. And given the two tanks of gas and the discount breakfast I had procured since my predawn rising, I was clearly on a roll. All things considered, it had been a pretty good day.

DAY 7: Fish or Cut Bait

"We Got no Gas
We Got no Lights
We Got no Heat
BUT WE GOT ELI!
GO GIANTS,"
— sign raised by a fan at the New York Giants-
Pittsburgh Steeler game, East Rutherford, New
Jersey, Sunday, November 4, 2012

For the record, I had every intention of running today
in the New York Marathon.

All that training shot to hell.

That's my story and I'm sticking to it.

Circumstances dictated another significant journey on
this brisk, sunny Sunday morning in New Jersey. We woke to
sub-50 temperatures in our home for the third day in a row
and that simply was not acceptable.

We had held out just about as long as we could. After
an hour in the Lexus seat-warmers and a short trip to the
shelter to recharge and freshen up, we revisited the issue of
our freezer-dictated soft deadline.

We examined the basement-freezer inventory and were
crushed to learn that conditions there had deteriorated
rapidly. The sustaining frost was gone, trickling from the
bottom of the unit in liquid form. The smaller items had
softened and that musty-fridgy smell was beginning to
establish itself.

It was probably too late for all but a few of the denser,
vacuum-packed meats, but it was clearly time to fish or cut

bait, especially since bait was probably all our jumbo bag of jumbo shrimp was good for at this juncture.

This would be a good time for some renewed perspective, because the dreaded decision we now faced had long-since been torn from the hands of so many people, especially down at the Shore. The decision to stay in their homes or leave was not theirs to make. They had been evacuated before Sandy came ashore and many of them, a week later, were still waiting for permission to go back.

Some of the barrier islands, however, recently had been opened to controlled, temporary reoccupation. Buses were hired to bring residents in, give residents a chance to assess or pack a few bags and bring them back to their temporary shelters. The bus trips also included some reporters and videographers who quickly posted the startling images of a coastline few of us still could recognize.

Some of those images, such as the roller coaster sitting in the ocean where an amusement park pier used to sit in Seaside Park, will stick with us to the grave. So will the images of streets, some of them several blocks from the shoreline, with up to four feet of sand deposited on the roadway in impassable dunes. In some cases, the sand actually had pushed through the windows of downtown shops and razed their shelves of inventory to sandy, soggy rubble.

Elsewhere, the buses were forced to detour around streets that had buckled either before or after the buildings they served had dislodged from their foundations to crash or crumble against the building next door. Boats were scattered everywhere, some in piles like the leaves on my front lawn.

It was Sunday and the first responders were working overtime. But the more we saw, and the more time that passed, the longer we imagined it would take to get us back to something resembling the old normal.

Lisa and I sat down and ran through the chosen contingency plan, which involved taking what was left of the perishables and heading to our waiting refuge in Easton. It also was time for me to admit to my wife — and myself — that I wasn't going anywhere.

Let me try to explain my determination to stay when there appeared to be little reason to do so. Quite certainly, there was some basic stubborn-male foolishness at play. Yet my reasons have deeper and more rational roots.

For one thing, we had been victimized by a burglar in 2010 and while there had only been a few reports of storm-related looting and such, I was worried about abandoning my dark home, on my dark street, with so many of my neighbors already gone. Our neighborhood, like so many, had turned into an all-night buffet for criminals smart enough to exploit the elevated vulnerability of their expanded pool of potential victims.

As a matter of fact, in a strange coincidence, our burglar, who was caught shortly after breaking into our home in July of 2010, had finally been sentenced to five years in prison the Friday before Sandy. We attended his sentencing — and his abrupt eviction from the cushy county lockup after two years of strategic sentencing delays — and banishment to the harsh state prison system the morning before the book launch for my second novel, "The Puddingstone Well" (this paragraph brought to you by www.onehitwillie.com, where both of my novels are featured and available for purchase, *hint hint*).

That had been quite an eventful day. It had been quite an eventful week.

But the feel-good vibes of the second Friday passed had been quashed by the reality we faced on this brisk, sunny Sunday morning. And it was time to share my reality with Lisa.

I had hinted about the option of her going and me staying without receiving much feedback, although I knew her natural inclination was for us to stay together. We were both better, not to mention safer, when we were together. And happier. Like sugar and salt, we were good on our own and irresistible together. We were the human manifestation of chocolate and peanut butter.

But I wasn't going anywhere. I explained this as diplomatically as I could and Lisa nodded her silent approval. She worried about leaving me to my own limited devices and frequent bull-headed stupidity, but she knew me well enough to know that changing my mind would be an exhausting and pointless exercise.

That and I think deep down, she had had it, and wanted out of our open-ended debacle. Was it too much to ask for a hot shower, a reading lamp and a warm bed?

I wanted these things for her as well, and I could not provide them here. I wasn't happy about the situation, not by a long shot, and I dreaded the prospect of a cold, celibate existence, much like the lonely Night's Watch guards on "Game of Thrones." I didn't want her to leave, but I needed her to, just as I needed to stay here.

Yeah, we were still among the lucky ones, but it was a difficult time as we emptied the freezer, packed the few keepers in a basket and placed it in her car.

We said our tearful good-byes, stating for certainty that the blackout could not last for much longer, and Lisa drove off.

She was replaced by another neighbor who had bugged out the first night and was back to inspect his castle. He was staying with in-laws and spoke of cabin fever, another trending phrase on social media. I had already heard from others how Sandy was making for some strange bedfellows and volatile family dynamics around the neighborhood. Crowded sofas, kids underfoot, clashing habits, that sort of thing.

Nothing violent, you understand, just another source of stress with uncertain expiration. *How long do we have to live like this?* If no answer is forthcoming, that leaves *forever* on the table. Think about that as you dine on boxed macaroni and cheese for the fourth straight night, while you wait for your cousin to finish watching "Dancing with the Stars," because he's sitting on the lumpy sofa you've slept on for five nights.

And you actually have to go to work tomorrow morning.

Yes, the signs of strain were beginning to show. I have one friend with a generator who had taken in his wife's parents, who were driving them crazy.

"I don't check the website to see if they are bringing power up in my neighborhood," he said. "What I need is for my in-laws to get *their* power back and get the hell out of my face."

My neighbor had lost some roof shingles and asked how our house came out. I said we were lucky, our old roof had held up. But from our current vantage point in the middle of the street, I could see that was not true. I took a closer look at my roof and could see a few shingles had, indeed, followed my window shutter and shed door off the property and probably into the next county.

I went inside to grab a pair of binoculars and returned to the street for a closer inspection. Two spots on the roof were exposed, not a lot, but enough to cause a leak, especially with the nor'easter now all but confirmed for Tuesday.

There wasn't a whole lot I could do but add a call to my insurance company on Monday. Having cleared the freezer — the refrigerator stuff went out with Friday's garbage pickup — I was about to make a list of the food we lost. Guess I would have to add roof repairs to the claim.

My business for the day concluded, I weighed my options for the afternoon. There was a Giants game about to start, which sounded like just the distraction I needed. Knowing my situation, I had several kind offers from neighbors and friends to share what warmth they had in their home. A few more with generator power invited me to come over and watch the game.

In the end, though, I chose to stay home and listen to the game on the radio. I was grateful that I had warm, friendly places to go if and when I really needed to, but the point of my staying was to *stay*. And I considered the cabin fever my friends were speaking of and realized that heat was not the only comfort in short supply at the moment. At least at home, I could have some peace, while visiting the home of others might add to their cabin fever or, more likely, expose me to their volatile conditions. I shuddered at the thought of watching the game with a buddy when his wife, or mother-in-law, would have preferred watching a movie on DVD. Or to have us outside raking leaves.

Nah, I would tune the game in on radio and watch it in my mind. The Giants are prone to playing ugly, so this way, I could use my imagination to airbrush what turned out to be a frustrating loss to the Pittsburgh Steelers at Met Life Stadium in East Rutherford, just a stone's throw from where a levee had breached in Moonachie less than a week before, causing floods throughout the low-lying Meadowlands region. The storm may have forced the cancellation of the New York Marathon — and train service to the stadium — but even Sandy didn't have the strength to scuttle NFL football.

The Steelers, by the way, had to fly in and out of town on game day because all the hotels were filled with displaced storm victims.

All kidding and tangential thinking aside, there was another reason for my determination not to abandon the ship, my home, the majority of my net worth. Standing your ground was in my DNA.

Before taking a bride on the cusp of the millennium — Lisa and I married on New Year's Eve, 1999 — I had spent close to fifteen years as the housemate of and primary caregiver for my Dad. A combat veteran of World War II, he was a simple man who asked for little more than a simple life in his own home.

71

He got us out of the deteriorating city of Paterson in 1961, happily accepting a forced buyout when the federal government pointed Interstate 80 straight through the living room of the two-story home we shared with my uncle and his family. Dad made sure his family landed on its feet in Parsippany, in the quiet, safe, kid-friendly neighborhood of Lake Intervale.

At age 70, with Mom passed some three years, Dad was diagnosed with throat cancer, a cruel blow to someone who never smoked in his life. I moved home shortly later, nursing financial wounds from a failed business venture, and we helped each other put our lives back together. He took the worst of it, enduring an assault of chemo and radiation therapy that miraculously did its job.

As the years passed, and Dad suffered more than his share of medical setbacks, I took on an increasing role as his primary caregiver. And as I spent more time with him, I was fortunate to get to know him better. One thing I learned about my Dad, and people like him who grew up during the Depression, is that their deepest fear is often the threat of being put out of their home. My Dad would tell stories of friends who, the last time he saw them, they were riding out of town on a horse-drawn cart with their family and what few possessions they had managed to hold onto.

They had been put out of their home by the banks.

Dad was mild-mannered by any measure, but when it was time for me to take over paying the household bills, he nagged me repeatedly not to ignore the property tax bill.

"Did you send the check yet?" he would ask. "They can take your house, you know!"

This from a man who spent more than two years following Patton through North Africa and Europe. Sleeping in muddy ditches and having Nazis shoot at you was one thing. Being put out of your home? That was something to keep you up at night.

As the temperatures continued their troubling descent in my house, I recalled with chilling clarity one night, a few years before my Dad died in early 1999, when our furnace died during a single-digit cold snap. I called for a repair visit and there were no appointments available until the next morning.

The house was freezing by sundown and, with my dad still recovering from a heart bypass, I wanted to find a warm spot to stash him for the night.

But he wasn't going anywhere. Sound familiar? See where I'm going with this?

A neighbor, his best friend, offered a vacant bedroom. *No dice.* Thinking perhaps he merely did not want to impose on his friend, I suggested the very respectable hotel right out on the highway, less than two miles away. *Nothing doing.*

In the end, I solved the dilemma with a fire circle of borrowed space heaters that I placed around his bed and watched over all night, as I have a deathly fear of space heaters. That particular phobia is rooted in life experience even more relevant than the reasons I am stating here for my fear-of-home-abandonment issues. But we'll leave them for another book. I've gone on about this for too long already.

The thing is, thinking about my dad would help to sustain me in the cold nights ahead. When times are tough, like they are now, I often think about my parents — charter members of the Greatest Generation — and the trials they endured living through the Depression and World War II.

Compared to them, and compared to the folks at the Shore, we were still lucky. Wish I was lucky enough to have my Dad still around, even if I would have had the same argument with him all over again. At least I was lucky enough to share his hearty DNA and could cling to his example should bad progress to worse around here, in the warm, happy home he bought his family to in 1961.

73

DAY 8: The Twelve Steps Not Taken

"The 800,000 or so we've restored is equivalent to four Hurricane Irenes," — John Miksad, senior vice president for electric operations at Con Edison, Monday, November 5, 2012

When a man finds himself in troubling times, he often leans on dangerous substances as a crutch. Left to my own devices and entertaining increasingly dark thoughts, I fell off the wagon and turned to a nemesis of my feckless, self-destructive youth.

That's right, dear readers. I slipped.

Hello, my name is Bill W. and I love fast food.

Hello, Bill.

It's OK now, though. I've been to some meetings and I haven't had a Big Mac or Whopper in two weeks.

Cue supportive applause.

Well, I did go to Five Guys, but no one can blame me for that. Be honest. You went there, too.

I'm getting ahead of the story here, which resumes the morning of Day 8. It was Monday and 6:30 a.m. In twelve hours, it would be exactly one week since Sandy rocked our world.

Unless, of course, they got the power back up before then.

Hah!

Right now, my breath was billowing like smoke through the crack of dawn peering in my bedroom window. The night and the bed were colder than ever, especially now that I was sleeping alone. When I rolled over at night, expecting the warmth of my Lisa, my arm fell across the empty expanse of our king bed, which had become a frigid, barren wilderness of Siberian-level permafrost.

The numbers? I slept in four layers of long sleeves under five blankets and a sheet. The temperature inside was 46 degrees, low 30s outside.

There still were nearly a million New Jersey homes and businesses without power and a like amount in New York. The JCP&L website, which I was now checking at least twice an hour, still showed about 380,000 customers off the grid, the majority of which were, naturally, in the Shore counties of Monmouth and Ocean, followed closely by my home base of Morris County, smack dab in the middle of North Jersey.

The JCP&L site also broke down the numbers by town and Parsippany — easily the most populous municipality in the county with about 50,000 residents — was at the top of the hit parade with just under 10,000 customers (out of 23,000) still offline. High percentages of outages could be found in the outlying townships in Randolph, Roxbury, Rockaway and Chester, where the roads were winding and the tree cover was dense.

As they worked their way into the neighborhoods, replacing poles and connections one-by-one, the progress had slowed considerably. Seven days into the crisis, we were now measuring the progress in weeks, not days or hours, although we were still checking the numbers by the minute.

Another set of numbers also was coming into play. The governor, responding to complaints that the utilities were offering no information on the schedule of power restoration, pointed us to a new website where we would find a spreadsheet that, town-by town, was offering a whole-number estimate of customers they expected to restore that day.

This spreadsheet, he said, had some of the information people were clamoring for. It was one thing to wait, and another to wait with no idea when you might expect relief. And the meteorologists were beginning to shake their heads again as they followed the nor'easter up the Atlantic coast to the shredded remnants of the Garden State.

Many of us eagerly typed the URL and, based on the real-time information on the outage site, the data appeared to be at least 24 hours old, with no indication that likely damage and delays from the nor'easter had been factored in.

Even worse, the numbers on the updated JCP&L spreadsheet were disappointing at best. The estimated restorations in Parsippany for this chilly Monday totaled 2,138, meaning about 30 percent of the township might still be dark for the next storm. Estimates for Tuesday (1,263) and Wednesday (945) set my odds of getting power back in the next three days at less than 50-50.

I needed a drink. Maybe two. There's another number for you.

Here are a few more significant numbers being factored on this last day of the 2012 presidential campaign, which had been simmering on the backburner of our subconscious: Obama 50 percent, Romney 49, or something like that. As I predicted, the president's unlikely bromance with our governor on the Jersey Shore had bumped up the incumbent's numbers a tick or two, although the election was clearly too close to call.

How the hell were we even going to vote? That was surely something to look into as I put my day together.

I had added the Parsippany Police Department and the mayor to my Facebook feed and both were posting some useful information. My first answer of the day popped up within minutes, as if they heard me thinking. My local voting site had been moved from the elementary school, which had no power, to the municipal building, which was running on generator power.

The mayor's page addressed another immediate concern of mine — hygiene. I had not taken a shower in two days and my hot-water heater at home had long since given up trying. Perhaps the mayor had read my mind again, or had caught a whiff of me when we bumped into each other at the shelter the other day. Hot showers, he told us, were available at the Parsippany Police Athletic League building. I grabbed a towel, several layers of fresh clothing and broke some local speed limits on my way to this hot-water oasis.

The joint was empty except for a cheerful white-haired gentlemen who was minding the front door. He guided me to the locker rooms, noting that "you just missed the mayor's wife, she was here for her shower." The mayor had told me the day before that his home was as dead as mine. I guess we were still in the same pickle today.

It was strange showering in such a large, unfamiliar and uninhabited space, where the large tile chamber seemed to echo every sound, including the spray of water on the floor. I remembered to bring a towel, but forgot soap and shampoo. Fortunately, I found some lying around and went about the work of washing away two days of stress and sweat with a sliver of soap no bigger than a flash drive.

It was glorious, though I wondered how glorious it would feel if I was still showering here a week from now.

Onto the community center, where I greeted some of now-familiar faces. This was my family now, at least my foster family. We had exchanged some names but I forgot them all. I have an uncanny memory for many things but names are not one of them. Among the friendliest faces in the group was a large family, originally from Kenya, who had been staying there for a few days. The family included two charming teenage kids who were polite, funny and full of questions.

There was a middle-aged Asian couple who, like me, had been coming and going, and a few other families with children who were trying to keep busy with laptop games and something resembling homework, although it had been a week since any of them had gone to school.

There were at least a dozen more individuals sleeping at the shelter. I became friends with one of them, Jane, a lady who appeared to be somewhere near my age. Her Texas-

77

Oklahoma accent gave me pause, but as we discussed current events, including the election, I was surprised to learn she leaned to the left, a rarity in my town, especially among those who speak with a Red State twang.

Turns out Jane was, among other things, a lyric writer, so we had our mutual interest in the performing arts to chat about as well. She was a recent transplant to Parsippany and, by coincidence, living in the neighborhood next to mine.

The conversation and the coffee were surprisingly good, but without my wife to anchor me, I was jumpy. For some reason, I was having trouble staying in one place for too long — perhaps because I just wanted to go home, microwave some popcorn, curl up in my warm, comfy chair and watch a ballgame on TV. None of those things were possible, so I kept moving, from the PAL to the shelter, back home and back into my car, with frequent trips around town in between, searching for signs that the linemen were coming to the rescue.

For the moment, there was very little evidence that my neighborhood would be next or soon. And on the radio, seven days after the lights when out, the utility companies seemed to be more in the dark than ever. They were still talking seven to ten days, maybe more, before everyone was back on the grid.

The word Thanksgiving even had crept into the power-restoration updates. *Thanksgiving?* I was still recovering from not having my power back before Halloween.

This nomadic existence became a pattern that would repeat over the next few days. Today, I added another stop to my route, a place called Fuddruckers. Fuddruckers is the upscale burger-chain joint on the highway near my home. Lisa and I had gone there in the past, although it never became a regular thing. I was always fascinated how Fuddruckers worked so hard to please everyone, with a big children's party room on one side of the dining room and a fully stocked sports bar on the other, like a Chuck E Cheese that had been retrofitted by Charlie Sheen. They even had a fully equipped ice-cream parlor.

Recently, the rather large establishment had been made over, with Fuddruckers pushed to one side to make room for another restaurant concept, Sonoma Chicken Coop. A corporate partner of Fuddruckers, Sonoma had just cut its ribbon and, as one of the few restaurants continuously open in town, it was having the Mother of all Grand Openings.

At this point, it was too cold even during the day to hang out in the house for any length of time, so I figured that a long lunch at a warm restaurant would do my chilly bones some good. I projected long-term and realized that if eating out was going to be a regular thing, I had best stay mindful of my fast-food-when-you-have-a-coupon budget.

Still, I was looking for warmth as much as comfort food and the dining rooms in the standard burger joints were drab and cold. The accommodations there were little better than my high-school cafeteria.

Since I was going stag, the bogo entrée coupon for Sonoma would do me no good. So I decided to see what they gone and done to my old Fuddruckers, and if the old girl could still bring the beef. The seating — I chose a booth in full view of a flat-screen TV — offered restaurant-quality comfort while the prices were reasonable, the food was above-average and I could get all this without having to leave a tip since there were no waiters.

The TV was tuned to pre-election coverage on Fox News. The sound was muted but you could see the look on their faces — their guy was in trouble. The swing states were turning as blue as a Kardashian sex video. Then I saw a clip of our governor hugging the president, which cut to the Fox hosts frowning and shaking their heads. After all the hyperbole, hysterics and vitriol, after all the billions of dollars spent on campaigning, it struck to me that the election might come down to a hurricane and two men hugging on the beach.

It also occurred to me that whomever we elected tomorrow as the leader of the free world, I hope he realized that he wasn't in charge of anything. Compared to what Mother Nature can do to us, Sandy was a swat on the rump. Mother Nature can take us behind the woodshed any time she likes, because she is Mom and she is in charge, and don't you forget that, Mr. Obramney.

Ah, we were talking about burgers, weren't we? And Fuddruckers makes a pretty good one, served on a soft, oversize bun with a farmer's market of fixings and gallons of condiments you can pump as you please.

Here's a tip: Don't mistake the horseradish-sauce pump for the mayonnaise pump.

They also had one of those space-age soft-drink dispensers that listed more than a dozen brand-name flavors on an interactive, touch-screen display. You could access supplementary flavors if you pushed the buttons and explored the sub-menus. There were four variations on grape soda alone, and four kinds of birch beer, regular-diet and sweet or sharp. I mean, God Bless America, right?

Oh, and one more thing. Are you sitting down for this? Because I have to sit just to write it: *The lunch special came with unlimited fries.*

The fools, I thought. *They don't know what I'm capable of.* I've already confessed on these pages to my french-fry fetish and I realize that without an intervention, they may one day lead to my ruin.

By the way, good copy editors know that proper style for french fry is lower case, so don't count the preceding as a typo. Not that we're counting typos, right?

And hey, no disrespect to the French, either. Really.

Presented with all these value-priced perks, I turned Fuddruckers into another base of operations for my evolving storm-contingency plan. I went at off-peak hours so as not to monopolize a whole booth during the lunch rush. Arriving somewhere between 2 and 4 p.m., no one seemed to mind my lingering, which at times bordered on loitering.

I was not alone, by the way. After a few days of return visits — I basically was eating one hearty meal per day — I began to recognize a few familiar faces, although we never took our relationship to the next level, meaning actual conversation. We were like-minded refugees, lured by the prospects of warm food, a warm dining room, a muted cable signal and unlimited fries.

As it turned out, I'm proud to say that I never once called Fuddruckers on their promise of unlimited fries. The first helping seemed to do the trick. It wasn't willpower or the risk of embarrassment to ask for more fried food, though. The truth of the matter was I really wasn't very hungry. Sandy had spoiled my usually reliable appetite. These were dark times, indeed.

DAY 9: Democracy in the Dark

"We may take a step back in the next 24 hours … you need to prepare for that," — Governor Chris Christie, Tuesday, November 6, 2012

With nearly 600,000 utility customers still without power in New Jersey, and millions more still reeling from Superstorm Sandy's impact, our society drew a line in the shifting sands and struck a blow for freedom on Tuesday morning.

Like NFL football, there still were a few inalienable rights beyond Sandy's influence. This was America, this was Election Day, and *screw you, bitch,* we were going to vote.

Tuesday morning began like the many preceding it, colder than the last one, probably warmer than the next. Only this morning, I actually had something to do. I planned to vote first and shower later at the PAL, but after a quick pit-whiff, I chose to reverse the order.

I had discovered a strange phenomenon under my covers: When bundling up beyond reason to sleep in the cold, you actually create a condition where you build up a sweat while sleeping under more layers than you'll find in an Elmore Leonard novel. So you wake up slightly ripened, to put it mildly. The cold-sweat phenomenon makes it that much harder to get out of bed, too. It was nasty enough without the added trauma of misguided thermoregulation adding a malodorous bite to the indoor frost.

An hour later, clean, fresh and casually dressed, I visited the Parsippany Municipal Building and its Council Chambers for the first time since Lisa and I were married there in a civil ceremony. This time, I pledged my commitment to the candidates of my choice. It was still early and the chambers were as warm as they were empty, so I announced my intention to vote very slowly. The election volunteers were not amused. I proudly accepted my "I Voted" sticker and moved on to the shelter to charge my phone and grab some of that hot municipal coffee.

I was surprised to learn that the community center also was a voting site. A partition had been closed in the large banquet room to separate the shelter-dwellers from the voters. There still was plenty of room, but I wondered if the shelter TV, loudly blaring election coverage, was some sort of violation of election laws. I kept that to myself, though. If they decided I was right and shut off the TV, it might have compromised the supportive relationship I had built with these poor fellow citizens.

While I waited, one of the inquisitive Kenyan kids, I'm guessing early-mid teens, asked me if I was voting and who was I voting for.

I smiled and replied that I had indeed voted, but that it was a secret ballot, and it would not be appropriate to reveal my choice, especially spitting distance from a voting site. Such a conversation might violate campaigning laws.

"I understand, but I'm a just kid and I'm trying to learn," she said, which nearly brought a joyful tear to my eye. I looked forward to the day she was old enough to vote, because I knew with that attitude, she would be ready.

"Tell you what, ask me again tomorrow," I said with a smile. "Assuming we're still here tomorrow, which I hope we aren't, but if we are, I promise to answer any questions about the election that you want to ask."

My next task was to research voting options for Lisa. Due to the fact that Sandy had driven so many residents out of their home, and in many cases out of state completely, New Jersey officials announced that an available email ballot provision — which existed for military-service personnel, among others — would be extended to anyone who had left the state. All I had to do was request the email ballot for Lisa and vote in her proxy, since Lisa is one of the 37 registered New Jersey voters who do not own a cell phone.

When I did not get an immediate automated response, I wondered if the government was prepared to pull this off. When I still had not received a reply after 90 minutes, I called Lisa and suggested she try the state's provisional ballot option. Displaced residents, we were told, could vote in any precinct, at least for the national elections, which this year included president and a senatorial race that was not expected to be competitive. Nor was the election for our birthright congressman, Rodney Frelinghuysen, who I assured Lisa would win by a wide margin regardless of her vote.

All that left on the ballot were three seats on the board of education (without school-age kids, we really did not have a dog in that hunt) and a seat on the Parsippany council, where a Democrat had not won in 30 years. So all things considered, crossing the Delaware from Easton to Phillipsburg to cast a provisional ballot seemed like the smart move.

Unlike the email ballot, the provisional ballot procedure worked like a charm. Reports surfaced later in the afternoon that the administrators of the email ballot provision had been overwhelmed by the response and were extending the deadline for email voting to Friday. For the record, we are still waiting for that ballot to show up in my inbox.

And wouldn't you know it? A Democrat won a council seat in Parsippany, even without Lisa's vote. We were living in interesting times.

From there, while America awaited the election returns, Mother Nature was returning to New Jersey for the second time in eight days. The nor'easter had swollen from rumor to fact and the forecasters were predicting 1 to 4 inches of heavy, wet snow and wind gusts in excess of 50 miles per hour. No biggie by nor'easter standards, but clearly something we could do without. The last thing we needed were more power failures or weather conditions that kept linemen out of their baskets, or more excuses for the utilities to revise their repair schedule downward.

I spent part of the afternoon at Fuddruckers, switching from the burger to the chicken sandwich. I watched Fox News in its morose, muted glory while the nor'easter announced itself in Parsippany with moderate winds and wet snow. The temperature was just above freezing and expected to stay constant well into the evening. I realized on the drive home that conditions would probably not encourage an evening trip to the shelter, so when I parked in my driveway, I stayed in the car a while longer to keep warm and finish charging the phone.

I thought about finally taking a neighbor up on his offer of shelter, then decided to stick it out. If the storm lived up to predictions, I was worried about damage to my home, wondering if Sandy had loosened any of my trees and if the nor'easter would be finishing the job. If the potential for damage wasn't enough to keep me home, the threat of sharing someone's cabin fever was. I just could not warm up to the thought of taking up space in the home of others who had been cooped up far too long with bored children, distant relatives and possibly other pathetic strays such as myself.

The prospect of facing a violent storm alone in a cold, dead house sounded pretty grim, yet somehow I felt largely unfazed by the whipping winds and accumulating snow. Perhaps I had been numbed by this point, perhaps my senses had been dulled by shock.

As the sun set, I was more preoccupied with the sight of a few first-responders who had been spotted in the vicinity. I drove back to one nearby point of interest — a tangle of downed trees, poles and lines on Morris Avenue in Mountain Lakes, which I was pretty sure was directly up the line from my substation power source. It was thrilling to see four line crews there, two of the men high above the ground in their cherry-picker baskets, ignoring the falling snow and doing their job.

I went back after dark for another visual update and they were gone, likely driven away by the increasingly sustained winds and gusts I estimated were beyond their threshold of 40 miles per hour. These were the kind of nor'easter delays we had worried about, but you really couldn't ask much more of these line guys. We have a JCP&L service depot less than a half-mile from our neighborhood and I had already seen dozens of linemen (I say linemen with accurate intent, having noted that female linemen were extremely scarce), most from out of state, sleeping in their trucks in a nearby parking lot.

This was the step back that nobody wanted to accept and the governor had warned us to expect. We still weren't listening. *Would you?*

Back home, with no reasonable hope of getting power back that night, I decided to do what we did during Sandy and try to sleep through the worst of it. Although Obama's victory was being predicted by every pundit to the left of Karl Rove, the outcome was not expected until after midnight. So I blew out the candles about 8 p.m., reached for a nap and hoped to wake up later to catch the speeches and analysis.

I did indeed wake up, sometime after midnight as memory serves, to hear that the major news networks had declared Obama the winner, although Romney was still putting off his concession speech. Again, for a journalist, I'm not very political. While I am a registered Democrat, my loyalty is more to the democratic process than the Democratic platform. Naturally, though, I was glad my guy won and took some small, needed comfort in the direction of this memorable Election Day.

Fine, you want my political opinion of the presidential race? Here it is: I voted for Obama's promise of hope and change four years ago and was disappointed in his performance. Am I better off than four years ago? Hell, no. I don't have a job. Neither does my wife. And if the Republican

Party had come up with a substantial candidate who they themselves could all agree on, I was eager to listen.

But please, my GOP friends, please don't tell me that Mitt Romney was the answer.

So there, just another predictable liberal rant from a tree-hugging pinko member of the so-called mainstream media. No big surprise, right?

Times like this, I always recall the old-school old-timer I was once paired up with at the municipal golf course. As we teed off, he noted with suspicion that I was left-handed. As we hit the back nine, I revealed in conversation that I was a writer and editor for the local paper, the Daily Record, which a lot of conservative folk refer to as the Daily Wretched.

As he saw another one of my drives slice into the woods, he remarked, "Considering what you do for a living, it's no wonder all your shots go left."

Everybody's a comedian.

DAY 10: Casual Wednesday, Part II

"A good day for America, I'm so glad we had that storm last week, because I think the storm was one of those things — not politically, I should say, not in terms of hurting people — the storm brought in possibilities for good politics." — Chris Matthews, MSNBC, Wednesday, November 7, 2012

We were trending downward, both as victims and as followers of the JCP&L restoration numbers. The number of people still without power had become a distinct minority, and the majority was desperate to get back to normal. I began to feel that if these outages lasted much longer, the powerless may come to be perceived as an inconvenience.

I was wrong about that — for the most part, anyway — but with the nor'easter and the election behind us, New Jersey's short-term distractions were being replaced with the need to re-establish some stability in the lives of as many people as possible. That meant putting the machine back in motion and getting society back into its recognizable routine.

Many businesses were opening and people were slowly getting back to work. At the governor's urging, schools were opening as well. Almost 600,000 customers — probably representing well over a million individuals — were still off the grid in New Jersey, but for the rest, it was *Ob-La-Di, Ob-La-Da, life goes on, brah.* Understandable, of course, but the prevailing winds here were turning against the likes of us who had been trapped for 10 days without power and were feeling that much more isolated this morning.

While the gears began to turn outside, we the afflicted bundled up, logged back on to the JCP&L site and fretted like stock brokers watching the big board during a stock collapse.

After cheering a power-restoration rally yesterday before the nor'easter, the numbers had gone back up overnight, to the point that on this second straight Casual Wednesday morning, we had lost nearly an entire day of progress.

I clung to my brave face and a veneer of calm, but it was getting frustrating. We were, in fact, imprisoned, with an open-ended sentence to our bread-and-water existence.

It becomes paralyzing after a while, the results of which range from sad to silly. You can't bring yourself to rake the leaves because you're too cold, too tired and it will be so much easier after a good night's sleep, a hot shower and a home-cooked dinner. And so it goes. You'll clean up that minute-steak grease when the power comes back on. You'll tie your shoe when the power comes back on.

I was caught in Sandy's vice-grip, waiting for some strangers in out-of-state power trucks to rise like angels in their baskets, above the lifelines of our humble shire, and bring the light back to our world.

Yeah, this was a new kind of crazy now.

You could feel it in the neighborhoods, too, as functional homes became encampments. The folks with generators were preoccupied with filling gas canisters to feed their hungry dragons, whose grinding drone had become as familiar as crickets in August. Fireplace owners who rarely stoked their hearths were scrounging for wood, while the dedicated natural warmers were out scoring a bumper crop of free firewood found on every roadside.

Meanwhile, I still was existing on the bottom of the new evolutionary ladder. No generator, no wood stove, no fireplace. Most of the people in my circumstance had long since joined the See-you-laters, so I was feeling more isolated than ever. Colder, too. I was beginning to doubt the sanity of my recent life choices, the wisdom of which I had long since abandoned.

Seriously, though, it was getting pretty damn cold. Having shared my situation on Facebook — and having several friends in similar or near-similar conditions — I was receiving suggestions here and there.

I had previously dismissed a suggestion to use my stove or my oven as a home-heating source. Hey, carbon monoxide and all that. Even a Boy Scout dropout knows that. But now the suggestion was originating from someone I knew to be a learned man, and he was adding a clever upgrade: boil big pots of water, which will result in more heat and, at least for a while, create a residual heat source that did not produce carbon monoxide.

Yeah, well, I know, still sounds pretty desperate, but I was really, truly getting desperate at this point. Thoughts about raking the leaves — or tying my shoe — had been replaced with a pinpoint focus on *how am I going to stay warm today, and what the hell about tomorrow?*

I still could just run and head for the comforting and by now fully defrosted arms of my wife in Easton. But I had come so far. How could I turn back now? It was Day 10, for Pete's sake. How much longer could it be? *(For the love of everything holy, don't answer that question.)*

Call it irrational, call it self-destructive, call it pride or what you will. I refused to leave my home. It's one thing if you do that under order of evacuation. As our governor has pointed out on several occasions, you risk the lives of first responders when you do that. I would never do that.

And I felt so bad for those who had been evacuated from their homes, felt worse for those who didn't have much of a home left to go back to. I felt so bad for these people, and admired the courage most of them demonstrated on the radio and in the news reports I read.

I sympathized with them and I admired them. But I did not wish to *be* one of them. And as long as I could stand it, I was going to complete this fool's vigil.

The storm had left a sloppy inch or two of wet, heavy snow on our fractured, cluttered landscape. The five-day forecast called for a merciful break in the unseasonably low temperatures. If we could last to the weekend, the snow would be gone and the sunny highs might crack the 60s.

To that forecast I tossed a favorite quote from former New Jersey basketball player Derrick Coleman: *"whoop de damn do."* There might not be much left of me by the weekend, and what was left probably wouldn't care anymore.

I surely needed a lift so I drove over to the shelter to charge up and check in on my new foster family, which had grown overnight as a few more families joined the See-you-laters during the storm.

The projection TV in the corner of the banquet room was tuned to the morning news which, of course, was blending election results with reports of both the nor'easter and Superstorm Sandy.

I chatted with Jane, who shared my satisfaction with the election results and agreed that most of our neighbors would be shaking their heads in disgust.

After some coffee and a bagel, paid for by my tax dollars, I turned my attention back to the TV. The news junkie in me was Jonesing for some video of victory speeches, concession speeches and high-tech analysis. Unfortunately, there were too many current events to give you comprehensive coverage of any one thing.

Apparently, the two Kenyan teens I had gotten to know (and I wish I could remember their names, even if I'm changing most of the real names in this book) agreed with me, in particular, the older, tall young man who had asked a lot of questions about our smart phones and laptops. He came to the shelter equipped only with an iPod that was either not working or he was bored with the music it stored.

He was a funny, inquisitive kid who had charmed me, Jane and several others in the foster family. Now he was eying my iPhone, which was sitting on the charging table.

"Is that your phone, sir?" he asked.

"Yeah," I said. I had an idea where this was going.

"You're not using it right now?"

No, I wasn't. But we had already been through this the other night. He wanted hip-hop. The closest I could come was James Brown and George Clinton, neither of whom he had heard of.

"Could I use it for a little while?"

"Sure," I said, hoping he might actually listen to — and learn to love — James Brown and George Clinton.

He sat at the charging table, plugged in his own ear buds and started pushing buttons. I resumed my conversation with Jane and we swapped information about signs of progress in our neighboring neighborhoods.

It was a short conversation.

While we spoke, I became increasingly curious about what the young man was finding so fascinating on my iPhone. I wandered over to see if I could get a peek at the screen.

He wasn't listening to music or playing games. He was on You Tube, watching videos of Barak Obama making his victory speech.

I looked across the room and saw the other teen — I'm guessing she was his younger sister — the one who had asked me the day before about who I voted for. I got up and went over to her.

"Remember what you asked me yesterday, about the election?" I said, getting a nod in response. "I voted for Obama."

"I was hoping he would win," she said. "I wish I could have voted for him."

"Well, a little more than half of the country agrees with you," I told her. "And half does not. Most of your town probably does not. Most of your county probably does not. Most of your state does."

She looked around the room, as though she was trying to figure out who voted with her and who didn't.

"Do you think they voted, too?" she asked.

"I hope so," I said. "And I hope when you are old enough, you will vote, too."

Her smile told me she would. I wasn't sure about some of the people in my new foster family, but the kids, they make us grownups proud.

The glow of my morning shelter visit quickly wore off as I made my morning reconnaissance of the neighborhood. I did not see any new damage from the nor'easter, but at 10 a.m., there were few signs of lineman back in my area. Why were they getting such a late start?

There were still more than 5,000 customers without power in Parsippany alone, representing about 20 percent of the township. A minority, granted, but still highly statistically significant, as the scientists say. *Come on guys,* I silently nagged the poor absentee linemen, who were probably trying to find something resembling breakfast after another night in a cab or on a cot. *Work to do!*

The predicted lows were in the 20s and even with the midday sun, the temperature in my house was only 50 degrees. The night ahead was plotting out as beyond tolerable levels, so I decided to give the water-boilng idea a dry run, if you'll pardon the pun.

An hour later, I had four large pots of boiling water and a thermostat reading 60 degrees. The experiment had been a smashing success, with one troubling side effect — condensation had invaded my home with a vengeance, and was dripping off windows, glass picture frames and even walls.

The humidity was a fair tradeoff and I made some adjustments to allow for the new New Normal conditions. I noted how the steamy heat rose efficiently to the top bedroom story of my split-level, and that by closing the other bedroom doors, I could direct a lot of the heat to my master bedroom.

I also made the bed, something I never do, because I could feel the sheets soaking up the steam and did not want to wrinkle in my sleep.

The house cooled quickly so I realized I would have to initiate another boil before bedtime. I fed from the Fuddruckers trough and returned to the shelter. The highlight of the evening was when the people running the shelter presented an ice-cream birthday cake to two young twin girls who were staying there with their parents. We all sang "Happy Birthday" to the happy kids, who were maybe 11 years old, and we all were served a small slice by the birthday gals. It was the first ice cream I had tasted in 10 days and, if you know me, that is an event so rare that the U.S. Mint should strike a commemorative coin.

Warmed by my frozen dessert, I went home and fired up the stove once more. Being a pragmatist, I planted myself at the kitchen table with my iPhone, a candle and the Little Black Radio, taking temporary refuge in the warmest room of the house. I covered my four layers of clothing with a dirty bathrobe — laundry surely was one of those things I would catch up on after power was restored — and managed to actually feel toasty in my home for the first time in more than a week.

My body was warm but my mind would not thaw. It was still in a dark, cold place. The idea that some unnatural heat should brighten my mood, well, the very concept mocked me at this point. I was like an insect, a lower life form that lived its life looking for food, warmth and another insect to mate with.

Again, I wasn't very hungry. And let's not forget where my mate was. So that didn't leave much.

This also was the point that I finally got sick and tired of hearing the same storm reports on news radio. All I wanted was information I could use. There wasn't much of that. The news cycle had moved more towards human interest, with poignant sound bites of storm victims crying about broken homes, flooded basements and sand where sand should not be.

The news on New York news radio was skewing more to New York as well, abandoning the Jersey Shore for the rising outrage on Long Island, where Governor Cuomo was throwing the astonishingly ineffective Long Island Power Authority under the bus, and the bus was not moving because no one on Long Island could find gasoline.

I didn't want to hear it anymore. I had my own problems, however many of them you might consider to be self-inflicted.

Enough was enough, so I moved the AM dial forward on the Little Black Radio in search of some entertainment. I also had lost my appetitive for games and even sports talk, but something else caught my ear. I tuned in to WABC radio and its near-suicidal roster of conservative talk hosts. One in particular, Mark Levin, was predicting a tax-and-spend world where right-thinking, white-skinned proper Christians were in the minority. So were his call-in listeners, some of whom were talking secession, some of whom were crying out with abject fear.

Somehow — and I'm not proud of this — I found comfort in their pain. Again, I'm not very political, and indeed had criticized many friends on both sides of the fence during the campaign for their slanted partisan rants. But now I was forming an odd kinship with another isolated segment of the population that, like myself, had stood its ground and freely chosen an uncertain path, a path that was now leading them to likely apocalyptic ruin. They could choose to be liberal and happy, but nothing doing. No one was going to remove them from the four walls they had built around them.

You can have my ideology when you pry it from my cold, dead hands, they seemed to be saying.

I may be at the bottom of the evolutionary ladder right now, I thought, but there are those who *have* to share my pain, and those who *choose* to share my pain. Either way, if I slip further, it was good to know there was someone down there to break my fall.

The candles blinked, casting unreliable illumination on my dangerously dark mood. I opened the camera app on my phone and flipped the lens perspective to see a fuzzy black shadow of myself, flickering like a silent movie in the fading candlelight, looking like Nosferatu wearing a fright wig.

I'd come close to the bottom before and was happy that I never stopped to take photos. Just for shits and giggles, I took one now, then deleted it a minute later. Maybe I would write a book about this experience someday and if this photo no longer existed, maybe I could use my skills for fiction to paint a prettier image of my unprecedented descent into hell.

DAY 11: The Hot-Stove League

"Township of Parsippany Update: [The mayor] has declared that the State of Emergency is officially over for the Township of Parsippany-Troy Hills.

"All traffic signals in the township are now functioning.

"Garbage, recycling and yard waste pickup is back on its regular schedule.

Schools are back in session.

"The Parsippany Water Department is off of generator and has had full electric power restored to all pump houses. State of New Jersey water restrictions are however, still in effect.

"JCP&L continues to work on restoration efforts within our township." — Parsippany Police Department Facebook post, Thursday, November 8, 2012

The cavalry was coming.

The scouts arrived first, in pickup trucks with flashing lights and cabs full of grimy men in reflective yellow vests. Some were trailed by other men in sedans, wearing suits and sporting the same out-of-state plates as the trucks in front of them.

They were waving; we waved back, suppressing the impulse to stop them and ask questions because we didn't dare slow them down. We knew why they were here. Why the hell else would an Ohio Edison truck be here in Parsippany on a school day?

So here were the out-of-staters who were going to help us while the rest of the township, county and state got back to their lives. Later that morning, charging up at the shelter, one of the staff came in holding a cell phone in front of her.

"The police say JCP&L will have crews in your section today and that power should be restored by the end of the day," she announced to Jane and I. Sweet Rosie O'Grady, was it possible that by tonight, we would regain our seat among the living?

I tried to corral my enthusiasm but I had to see for myself. I drove back home and cruised around the local neighborhoods. There were crews in four of them, two hard at work; two others, including one around the block from my house, were just standing around.

These guys, who were from Chicago, actually spoke with us. They were waiting for some repairs to be completed somewhere up the grid and the signal to start working on our lines.

They were understandably skittish about promising anything — they knew how desperate people were, and how difficult this restoration still was — but it was still the most hopeful and positive sign we had received in nearly two weeks.

I logged onto the neighborhood intranet, the one where neighbors gather in the streets. Others had been talking to linemen here and there and we were comparing notes on what we heard from them and elsewhere. Rufus was skeptical about the police announcement, but I said the mayor and police were so hesitant to offer false hope at this point that they must be pretty sure about this.

Still, I had to keep my head and think about what might happen if the darkness lingered for another night. The water-boil had gotten me through the night — although by morning, it was back to 46 degrees inside and I was worried about the condensation. Some of it had literally melted dirt off a few glossy-white-painted doors, which had creepy, greasy, streaky stains gathered at the bottom. One more boil, I worried, might promote the kind of unhealthy mold growth that Shore residents were dealing with.

I mentioned this to Rufus, who said he had a 20,000 BTU kerosene space heater I could borrow. The very idea of a space heater with an actual open flame frightened me out of my dirty socks, but so did the prospect of another night of sub-freezing slumber.

We dug it out of the back of his garage workshop and I recognized it immediately. It was one of the space heaters I had borrowed to keep my dad warm that night when our furnace had died. It was round and monolithic, with a wide base that held the kerosene, a stove-like burner and a large cylindrical chamber on the top.

"Remember, you have to keep a window open, but I'll bet it can warm a good portion of your house," he said.

We fired it up and it seemed to work just fine, even though I suspected it had not been used since I borrowed it about 15 years ago. I wondered if the kerosene also was that old. Not that it mattered. I was up for anything that might produce heat at this point.

The heater worked reasonably well, not as fast or effective as the water-boil, just a lot dryer. There was no way I would leave it on unsupervised or overnight, but if I ran it well into the evening, it might buy me another day.

Sadly, I would need that extra day because predictions of our restoration faded with the daylight. My bitter disappointment was exceeded only by that of the conservative voices on talk radio, which I found myself listening to once again at my kitchen table in the flickering shadows of exhausted candles.

I expressed some of that sadness on Facebook, where I tried to keep my upper lip stiff with some whimsical humor. It came out in lyrical form, with a melody borrowed from a previously mentioned Beatles song, "Ob-La-De, Ob-La-Da":

Ob-La-De, Ob-La-Da, lights go on?
Nah!
Nah-nah-nah no lights go on

Then I completed the medley with another track from the White Album, the salacious "Why Don't We Do it in the Road?":

My power line is in the road,
my power line is in the road,
no one wants to rescue us,
my power line is in the road

You had to laugh, to keep from crying.

The dry heat, though, managed to comfort my lonely despair, so before I went to bed, I turned the dial on the Little Black Radio back to sports talk. Bless that Little Black Radio, it was operating on the same four AA batteries it had been stored with.

The chat was all about baseball trades and free-agent signings, an offseason pastime we old-school baseball fans commonly refer to as the Hot Stove League. I smiled to realize I had my own Hot Stove League going at the moment. The water-boil was strictly amateur, while the jumbo space-heater had vaulted me into the professional minor leagues. I could only hope that tomorrow, someone would punch my ticket to the bigs.

DAY 12: The Bunny-Boil Advisory

"I'm not going to be ignored, Dan!" — Glenn Close to
Michael Douglas, "Fatal Attraction" (1987)

I understood the need for most people to attempt a
return to normalcy.

What I could not accept was a government that went
along with the charade.

You already know I am long-winded, so it should not
come as any surprise that I am a squeaky wheel. Not a chronic
complainer, you understand, only that when I see something
being done the wrong way, I speak up.

So many elected officials, public servants and
volunteers had stepped up since Superstorm Sandy tilted our
axis. And this recovery broke new ground in terms of the
unexpected, so some mistakes and setbacks had to be
expected along the way. As I watched and waited, I had
observed many of those errors, some more costly than others,
but I held to my firm belief that we all had to keep a cool head
and support the efforts of those tasked with resuscitating our
community.

I managed to keep my squeaky wheel oiled until this
morning, this Day 12 of my Superstorm Sandy journey, which
began with an early trip to the shelter. The first thing I noticed
was that the signup desk was unmanned. They had been
pretty strict about signing in and out, even folks like me who
were constantly coming and going.

I wanted to track down Jane to ask if her section had
gotten power back overnight. She wasn't there. No one was
there.

I went down the hall to the offices of the community-
center staffers who had been caring for us all this time and one

of them said the shelter was being closed down. If we still needed services, we could go to the Red Cross shelter on the other side of town at the police academy.

Say what? I said to myself, sparing the angelic staffers who had made us feel so welcome and added that I was welcome to stay, at least for today.

Say what? There were still thousands of us in Parsippany, tens of thousands in Morris County and several hundred-thousand of us in the Tristate region still flopping around like flounder on a fishing boat.

Twelve days of patience had come to an end. For way too many of us, the crisis was far from over. We had been all but promised our power would be back last night and it wasn't. Which made any predictions about today or tomorrow worth less than the paper they were written on.

Yet the mayor had declared the state of emergency over yesterday, and was closing the shelter today.

In retrospect, the mayor was probably doing the right thing. After the nor'easter, shelter residents had mostly dispersed. Only a few people were using it, and the Red Cross was right in town, so closing the township shelter, at least on paper, was clearly warranted.

But *I* had been using it, *I* had been patient, *I* had been a grownup about everything for 12 days, and now they were closing the shelters while continuing to state that everything that could be done for the victims was being done.

"Doing everything they can? Don't pee down my back and tell me it's raining," I told Rufus, the first innocent target of my frosty melt-down.

My anger grew as I went back to my freezing house, which I had not yet abandoned but was no longer speaking to. We really, really needed to spend some time apart, I concluded, and might have to look into dweller-dwelling counseling down the road.

It was just about high noon, a good a time as any for a showdown. I took to Facebook and posted my outrage:

Bill Westhoven
Like . Comment . 1 minute ago near Parsippany

They shut down the shelter at the Parsippany Community Center. Even though there's still as many people without power in Parsippany and Morris County as there were two days ago. I guess they are tired of the whining and we should just get back to our lives. I've been patient up to now but to quote Glenn Close, "I'm not going to be ignored." *Time to go boil a bunny.*

You know the movie and you know the scene, right? Fine, let's move on.

My uncensored intentions declared via the metaphorical bunny-boil advisory, I proceeded to issue similar missives of outrage on the Facebook pages of my mayor, my congressman and even my police department, apologizing to them but urging their continued vigilance while the crisis was still alive and well in their township, despite some circumstantial evidence to the contrary.

My cathartic rants did little to soothe my rage, my nerves, my tattered spirit. I wondered again, how the hell was I going to make it through another day of this crap?

I wasn't sure what to do next when the power suddenly came back on. It started with a click here, a click there, followed by the whir of the hard drive on my cable box.

I squeezed my eyes tightly shut, fearing they would refuse to confirm what my ears were hearing. Then I heard the most wonderful sound I had ever heard: The furnace burner kicked in with a whoosh, followed by the smooth whirl of the furnace fan.

I slowly opened my eyes and saw the cable box display sequencing through its reboot — *hold, hold, hold … turn on!"* I did as instructed and was rewarded with the closing scene of "The View." The ladies looked and sounded very happy.

Not as happy as the Rib King.

103

I ran down to the basement to inspect the furnace, which seemed to be running at peak efficiency. I read the label on my hot-water heater to light its pilot and bring me hope of a hot shower.

Then I ran back upstairs to turn on the oven. There was no telling how long the power would stay on, so I wanted to make sure every heat source in the house was making a contribution while it still could.

Half an hour later, the house was up to the low 60s and the temperature was climbing rapidly, I removed two layers of clothing and called my wife with the good news. We agreed that it might make sense for her to stay in Easton for one more night, just in case we were cut off and detoured back to the stone age.

Finally, I allowed myself to relax and collect my thoughts. And the one thought I kept coming back to was *Damn, I finally stopped being patient, guillotined my cool head and within an hour of posting rants, rage and metaphorical threats involving helpless animals, they give me back my power.*

So much for being a mature grownup. Next time, I vowed, no more Mr. Nice Guy.

... And The Days That Followed

"I was worried I was going to come out here and get angry with you, but this is nice" — Governor Chris Christie, to Seth Meyers during the "Weekend Update" segment of "Saturday Night Live," Saturday, November 17, 2012

Lisa came home early Saturday morning and we happily closed the books on our longest separation since well before our marriage. Both of us were exhausted, physically and emotionally, and Lisa probably wanted to just clean up the house a little and spend some quality time with her own bed.

I, on the other hand, needed to get out, and my best friend had invited us over to share lunch and watch the Rutgers-Army football game. Lisa, as always, was sympathetic with my needs. It helps that my best friend is married to her best friend, so off we went, trying to gather some long-overdue normal into our disrupted lives.

Our friends live some 25 miles to the south, in Somerset County, which also took its share of wind damage. Our friends had gotten their power back just a few days before us, although they had a generator and a wood stove, both of which they shared with family for more than a week.

The ride south along Interstate 287 was, putting it mildly, an eye-opener. The forested region between the counties had been partially harvested by Sandy. The land looked like she had scraped through it with her fingers. Long lines of flattened trees could easily be distinguished from one another, the trees leaning on each other like fallen dominoes in some places; broken, mangled and twisted in others.

In between, other trees stood as they had for decades. Sandy had plowed their fields in angry, jagged rows, leaving scars that would take years, even decades, to heal.

Certainly the Jersey Shore no longer looked like the festive path to a summer-vacation past and present that we all cherished. As I complete this story, on November 23, I still have not heard a word about our favorite Jersey Shore destination, Sandy Hook, which is part of the federally operated Gateway National Recreation Area. All I know is that the towns of Sea Bright to the south, and Keansburg to the mainland west, both suffered devastating damage.

Shortly after Hurricane Irene passed last year, Lisa and I drove down to Sandy Hook to inspect our usual beach. We knew our beach well enough to see that Irene had made profound alterations to the shoreline, and we marveled at the incredible power wielded by Mother Nature.

We haven't yet had the time to visit Sandy Hook since Sandy came and went. I've been busy writing a book, you see.

To tell you the honest truth, I'm not sure our beach is even there anymore. The ocean met the bay in many places along the Shore. I fear Sandy Hook was among them.

As time passes, we'll get the answers to all these questions and more. More time will pass and most of us, no doubt, will really and truly get back to normal. Maybe the president will use his modest mandate to create jobs and improve the economy, maybe we'll even get back to work and no longer have time to write books.

But too many of us will still be homeless, jobless and hopeless long after this book is published. Like the governor said, the Jersey Shore we knew may never look the same as we remember it. Likewise, many residents of the Shore are forced to face a crossroads in their existence. Most of them, I hope and pray, will go on to bigger and better things, at the Shore or elsewhere, but going back to the way things were is no longer an option.

This is why I chose to write and publish this book as quickly as possible, to offer a snapshot memoir of my own Superstorm Sandy experience and put it out there — *right now* — when and where it can do the most good. If the immediacy of my story helps to sell more books and raise more funds for storm relief, then so much the better.

Other books documenting Superstorm Sandy will no doubt be published in the coming months and years, and for more detailed information about this unforgettable event, a quick Google search will give you plenty of facts, analysis and numbers to crunch at your leisure.

I have included some facts, quotes and numerical analysis on these pages but this story is something different. I'll leave Sandy's bigger picture to others. My goal was to offer my narrow, unvarnished and unremarkable experience and let you share the viewpoint of a regular Jersey guy in a typical post-Sandy mess, before it has had time to cool, congeal and lose its pungent honesty.

It's the literary equivalent of a Facebook post that you may or may not regret posting somewhere down the line. I'm willing to take that risk if I can make a difference in some small way.

Call this story — published just 30 days after Superstorm Sandy left us — an experiment in the untapped potential of modern self-publishing. I hope I was able to capture the moment and that sharing it does you some good. If not, well, at least you will have contributed to a worthy cause, and I am profoundly grateful for your participation.

See you on the Boardwalk!

ABOUT THE AUTHOR

A former mobile disc jockey, voiceover artist and Crazy Eddie store manager, William Westhoven was a full-time journalist from 1989 to 2011, when he fell victim to newspaper industry-wide layoffs.

Since then, he has branched out to fiction, writing and publishing two complete novels. "One-Hit Willie," a historical novel that covers 50 years of music in America, was released in December of 2011. "The Puddingstone Well," a contemporary mystery-fantasy, was released on Oct. 26, three days before Superstorm Sandy hit the Jersey Shore.

Westhoven began writing "Superstorm Sandy: A Diary in the Dark" three days after getting power back to his home on November 9, 2012. He spent the 12 days before that in his home without power or heat.

Written and released within a month of Sandy's departure, "Superstorm Sandy: A Diary in the Dark" is the first published book to document the devastating storm and its initial recovery period.

The author pledges to donate all paid royalties from the sale of this book to the nonprofit Hurricane Sandy New Jersey Relief Fund.

During his newspaper career, Westhoven earned several national and state awards for writing, editing and page design. His theater column, Morris Stage, ran for nine years in the Daily Record and, as a performing-arts critic, he earned seven first-place awards for Critical Writing from the New Jersey Press Association.

Westhoven's first book, "Eric Clapton: Career of a Rock Legend," was published in 1996. In between his book projects, he continues to work as a freelance journalist, with recent work appearing in several newspapers and Patch sites, the Huffington Post and Guitar World Online.

For more information, visit www.onehitwillie.com.